How to Make a Living Trading Foreign Exchange

Founded in 1807, John Wiley & Sons is the oldest independent publishing company in the United States. With offices in North America, Europe, Australia, and Asia, Wiley is globally committed to developing and marketing print and electronic products and services for our customers' professional and personal knowledge and understanding.

The Wiley Trading series features books by traders who have survived the market's ever-changing temperament and have prospered—some by reinventing systems, others by getting back to basics. Whether a novice trader, professional, or somewhere in-between, these books will provide the advice and strategies needed to prosper today and well into the future.

For a list of available titles, please visit our Web site at www.WileyFinance.com.

How to Make a Living Trading Foreign Exchange

A Guaranteed Income for Life

COURTNEY D. SMITH

WILEY

John Wiley & Sons, Inc.

Published by John Wiley & Sons, Inc., Hoboken, New Jersey.
Published simultaneously in Canada.

For general information on our other products and services or for technical support, please contact our Customer Care Department within the United States at (800) 762-2974, outside the United States at (317) 572-3993 or fax (317) 572-4002.

Wiley also publishes its books in a variety of electronic formats. Some content that appears in print may not be available in electronic books. For more information about Wiley products, visit our Web site at www.wiley.com.

Library of Congress Cataloging-in-Publication Data:

Smith, Courtney, 1952–
  How to make a living trading foreign exchange : a guaranteed income for life / Courtney D. Smith.
        p. cm. — (Wiley trading series)
  Includes index.
  ISBN 978-0-470-44229-6 (cloth)
  1. Foreign exchange market.   2. Foreign exchange futures.   3. Investment analysis.
4. Risk management.   I. Title.
  HG3851.S59 2010
  332.4′5–dc22

                                                              2009031709

Printed in the United States of America

10 9 8 7 6 5 4 3 2 1

To my parents and my foxhole buddy

Contents

Preface

T rading foreign exchange (forex) is one of the most exciting and potentially lucrative activities in the world. Yet about 90 percent of traders lose money. This book is designed to create *profitable* traders.

Can you make a living trading forex?

Yes!

And no.

Let me explain.

It is common wisdom that about 90 percent of traders lose money trading forex, about 5 percent break even, and about 5 percent make money. I have not seen any scientific evidence that this is true but I have talked to senior executives at brokerage houses and they tell me that this is a rough guide to what happens to traders. My own experience as a senior executive in the futures and options industry also confirms the same dreary results.

There was a study by the federal government back in the 1960s of futures traders and they found that futures traders had those same statistics. However, the underlying data were not so dismal.

It was true that 90 percent lost money, but that was *after* commissions. They actually had about a 7 percent return on their investment before commissions. The main reason that they were losing was commissions. The theory back then was that the 7 percent gain was the equivalent of an insurance premium that commercial companies paid to speculators to take over the risk of the commercials. Trading forex does not incur any commissions (and futures commissions are much lower now) so I doubt that this factor is so important anymore.

However, forex does have other transaction costs in the form of the bid/ask spread. The cost of buying at the ask and selling at the bid on every trade is a significant drag on performance over a given year.

Let's assume a $10,000 account trading mini-contracts. Let's further assume that there is a 3 pip bid/ask spread for each trade. Now assume that we do almost one trade per day, or 250 trades per year. That comes to a $750 expense off the top of trading. We have to overcome that vig each year to make a profit. We effectively start out in the hole by 7.5 percent when we start the year trading. We need to make at least 7.5 percent profit just to break even.

I think those assumptions are similar to many traders'. Take a look at your own experience to see where you stand and how much headwind you have to overcome to break even.

It might actually be worse than that. The most common form of forex trading is spot forex through a retail forex broker such as FXCM or Sterling Gent. Brokers take an additional profit from the roll every day. I'll explain what the roll is in Chapter 1, but please note that brokers effectively take a bid/ask spread every day. This is worth another, say, $3 per day per open position. Let's assume that you only have on one position per day and that adds up to another $750 per year. We are now up to a 15 percent headwind to make any money. Stock investors tend to make money but that is largely because the stock market drifts higher over any decent, long period of time, not because stock investors are better investors. In addition, there is no time limit when you invest with stocks. Futures and options expire. Forex doesn't expire but the high leverage keeps people from hanging on to positions for years the way they can with stocks. Investors will often hang on to losing positions in stocks for years waiting for them to return to profitability. That is technically possible in forex, but it's rarely done.

The high leverage creates a mentality toward trading that works against traders. Basically, trading forex attracts a "get rich quick" mentality that works against the trader. Contrast this mentality with the normal stock investing mentality that looks to buy and hold.

The pressures of dealing with high leverage cause the usual forex trader to make a lot of mistakes. And those mistakes cost more than in the unleveraged stock world. The high leverage puts a lot of mental pressure on the forex trader that is simply not there in as high a degree for a stock trader.

The sum of all these differences is that the forex trader has a much harder time making money than a stock trader. But . . .

The subtitle of this book is *A Guaranteed Income for Life*. This title was inspired by an infamous poker book from 20 years ago. I truly believe that the material in that book can create a guaranteed income for life. This is not BS. Here's what it requires: *You must do exactly what I say to do in this book. You must not deviate. You must execute flawlessly. Only after you have mastered this material should you start to be creative.* This self-discipline is critical to your success. A lackadaisical attitude will put you back in the category of a losing trader. You and I both don't want that to happen.

I can't repeat it enough: Execute the plan in this book and you will be a profitable trader. You will live a life that few can even comprehend.

I wrote much of this book while hanging out near the beach in Belize. I'm writing this Preface on a plane to Singapore where I will first give a speech to about 2,200 people and then relax in several Asian countries in beach houses.

How can I do this? Internet access. That's it. I do all my analysis and trading online. I can't live in the real boondocks because I need Internet access but I can live a remarkable lifestyle anyway. My first stop after the Singapore speech is a week in Bali.

Guess what? I don't even really need constant Internet access. I really only need Internet access for about 15 minutes a day. I prefer more than that because I post a lot of instructional videos on my educational Web sites and that takes more time and bandwidth. But how about just a few minutes at an Internet café in China or London or wherever? That's all I need. The true goal for me, and most people trading forex, is not to make a lot of money but to gain *freedom*.

I know that I presented a rather dismal picture about how hard it is to make money in the forex world. But I'm not only saying that you will make money, I am also saying that you can have a guaranteed income for life. This is a very strong statement.

How do I know that this is true? How can I be so sure?

I have spent many years training traders. I have been teaching these techniques for over 25 years. More important, I have been training retail investors with no experience at all trading let alone trading forex. It has been a very gratifying experience. I have really enjoyed watching people create a new life for themselves. Every single one of my retail educational clients has made money trading forex, except one. (And he is down just a little.)

At one point, I foolishly offered a mentoring program called Extreme Profits. This was a short but intensive program that I charged $2,000 to take. Here's the insane part: I offered a money-back guarantee if students didn't double their money in a year. What an idiot I am!

All but one student doubled their money. These were normal retail investors; no trading pros in the group. The one woman who didn't double her money asked for her money back and I gave it to her. By the way, *she was up 70 percent for the year*.

So I know that it can be done. I know that you can do it!

But (isn't there always a but?) you must execute flawlessly.

That's it. That's the secret.

Now go through this book. Execute the plan. Make money. Live the life you dream about.

OVERVIEW OF THE CONTENTS

I've designed this book to be useful for anyone who is interested in making money trading forex, from novice to pro.

This book explains all the basics that a novice needs to know to get going. At the same time, experienced traders will find the systems and methods, particularly my enhancements of classic methods, to be of significant value. Every trader will find the sections on the psychology of trading and risk management will sharply enhance their profitability.

Chapter 1 outlines the basic information you need to get started in trading forex. Perhaps you've traded stocks or mutual funds or even futures. But I assume that you know nothing about trading forex. I've also included a number of real stories of my trading, to give some flavor of the life of a professional institutional trader. Even if you have some experience trading forex, this chapter is worth reading for the examples.

Chapter 2 is where we really start the methods of making money in the forex market. This chapter introduces trend analysis. This technique is similar to what have been called 123s. However, I add in a unique method to truly define which trends to jump onto and which ones to sidestep. In addition, I introduce to the public for the first time the Bishop technique. This unique indicator has a tremendous track record of getting out of trades at major highs or lows. It doesn't give a lot of signals but you should pay very close attention when it does. I will exit all my open positions on any technique whenever I see a Bishop buy or sell signal. It's that powerful.

I'm also introducing in this book a new way to filter trades. This filter eliminates about half of my losing trades while only eliminating about 5 percent of my winning trades. What a great tradeoff! It dramatically enhances the profit of the trend analysis and other techniques.

Chapter 3 is all about channel breakouts. This classic technique has been around since the 1960s. It's been around that long because it is that profitable. I'd estimate that most of the largest and most profitable forex hedge fund traders are using some variation of this technique. However, I introduce several major enhancements to the classic technique that turbo-charge the profitability.

The first enhancement is the principle of instant gratification, which is an underlying principle that will show you how to greatly enhance your understanding of the market, how to profitably trade, and how to boost your profits. I also introduce the rejection rule. This powerful enhancement cuts the risk of trading channel breakouts by at least half, yet it retains all the profit potential. It basically monitors the health of a breakout and leaps out of the position if there is no follow-through. In addition, it cuts down on the psychological stress of trading channel breakouts. The concept behind the rejection rule can be applied to other trading methods. You won't want to miss this idea. I then add in another exit strategy called the last bar. I got this idea from ace trader Peter Brandt. It sharply reduces the risk in any given trade to a trivial amount. As you can imagine, cutting risk to small amounts dramatically enhances your profits at the end of the year.

I introduce the Conqueror in Chapter 4. This is a truly unique trading system that was originally designed by legendary trader/analyst Bruce Babcock, enhanced by ace system researcher Nelson Freeburg, and finally tweaked by me. This system monitors the market from three different time perspectives and doesn't enter the market until all three are calling for an entry into the market. Another unique feature of this method is that it uses different exit techniques than the entry techniques. This is the only method I know that uses different exit and entry techniques.

The Conqueror is a technique that has a very hard time entering the market. It wants all the conditions to be perfect before entering a trade but jumps out of the position at the slightest intimation of weakness in the trade. I love this system and I think you will, too!

Chapter 5 introduces how to use stochastics profitably. It seems like everybody uses stochastics; they are perhaps the most popular indicator in chart services. Yet everyone is using them *wrong*. This chapter shows you how to profitably use stochastics while sidestepping the usual traps that drain money from your account. I show you how I use stochastics to identify short-term turning points and, more important, how to identify major turning points. As a bonus, I have included an amazing interview with the inventor of stochastics, George Lane. I had the privilege of interviewing him before he passed away. This hard-hitting interview reveals how he invented stochastics, where they got their name, and, most important, how George himself used stochastics to make money in his trading. He literally states that, used correctly, "it is damned near infallible"! This interview is priceless.

Another unique feature of this book is that I show you different profitable techniques to use over different time horizons. The techniques discussed here are techniques that look at the market from the perspective of days to weeks. Chapter 6 introduces several techniques that trade over a much shorter term. These techniques hold positions for less than one day. These pattern-recognition techniques are great for those traders who want to make money during the day rather than over the next week or month. I like to think about these trades as just churning out some nice profits day after day. No monster profits because you can't make monster profits in just a day. But making a nice chunk of money during the day is a very nice thing.

This chapter also introduces the multiunit tactic. This technique uses multiple contract positions to give you more flexibility in your exits.

This technique has a lot of positive psychological benefits while also giving a kick to your profits.

You cannot control the profit you make unless you control the risk in your account. You are doomed to losses if you don't control the risk in your account. Ninety percent of forex traders lose money while only about 5 percent make money. I argue that one of the critical differences between the winners and the losers is that the winners know how to control the risk in their account.

Chapter 7 drills down on this important subject and gives you clear instructions on how to control the risk in your account to ensure that you will be a profitable trader. I even take risk management one step further and show you how to use it as an offensive weapon, not just a defensive one. The concept of using risk management as a method for enhancing profits is rarely talked about in the markets. This chapter is critical because you need to be able to survive the inevitable losing streaks without losing any significant money and to also be able to maintain the proper mental state. You must never get to a situation that is both financially and mentally debilitating.

The next chapter, Chapter 8, shows a new technique called the Slingshot as well as the mini-Slingshot. I also use this chapter to extend the discussion of risk management. The Slingshot is a very interesting chapter due to the unique concepts embedded in it. It builds on the risk management concepts from the previous chapter.

I believe that risk management is actually the second-most important factor for investment success. Chapter 9 looks at the biggest block against making money in the markets: *you*. It is your psychology. You are the biggest problem. Intellectual skills are trivial. You will rarely have problems with the methods that I present in this book. The basic risk management rules are also easy to apply. But the psychology of trading is intense and few can master it. I want you to be a huge success; it is the real key to making money in the market. Please do not disregard it or push it to the side. I am laying out a lot of profitable techniques in this book. But you will not make any money with them if you don't have the proper psychology. For example, what good is a profitable method if you don't have the self-discipline to execute the trades on a daily basis? You will fail. You need to be able to execute the techniques or the techniques are useless.

I am a big believer in stress-free trading. Why should I trade if I get all wound up in stress while doing it? I may make money but I shouldn't trade if the stress is overwhelming. Life is too short. Once again, we need to deal with the psychology of trading.

This chapter goes into the reasons people trade. No, it's not just to make money. I also go into all the reasons that people lose money and show specifically how to overcome those reasons. There may not be any sex appeal in dealing with our own psychology but it is the most important factor for trading success.

Chapter 10 shows you how all these techniques fit together. By this point, I will have shown you a collection of powerful techniques for making money trading forex. This chapter shows how they all fit together into a coordinated program for profits. Each technique has a different purpose from the other techniques. So the totality of the techniques is truly greater than each technique separately. Once again, this is a very unique approach. Most books will present techniques but no framework.

You should come away from reading this book with a concrete and comprehensive approach to making money trading forex. You will have a toolbox full of profitable techniques. You will understand how to manage your risk. You will understand how to have a stress-free psychology of trading. Good luck!

How to Make a Living Trading Foreign Exchange

CHAPTER 1

The Basics of Foreign Exchange Trading

F oreign exchange is the most traded instrument in the world. Roughly $3 trillion is traded on any given day. Some days, volume can reach as high as $7 trillion per day. This volume completely swamps the global stock market.

It is not hard to understand why forex is traded the most. Nobody needs to buy stocks but we must all deal directly or indirectly with the foreign exchange (forex) world. Global trade is huge. Every time a barrel of oil is bought, dollars must also be bought by everybody but Americans. Japanese must change their yen into dollars to buy oil since oil is priced in dollars. Every time an American buys a Japanese car, dollars are swapped for yen to buy the car. Every time a kid watches a Disney movie in Poland, dollars are demanded. Cross-border capital flows for investment contribute another massive quantity of foreign exchange transactions.

Perhaps the largest component of daily volume is speculation. This is mainly done by banks and other financial institutions around the world. Every day, banks trade among themselves looking for speculative profit. In addition, major banks try other strategies to make money. For example, a bank will try to find another bank that doesn't know the correct price for a currency and make a purchase. Perhaps a large order had come into a bank that was large enough to change the price of the currency. This piece of knowledge could create additional profit opportunities for the bank that knew about the order. This will be discussed later in this chapter. Let me assume that you know something about investing in general, perhaps in stocks, and focus on how the forex market is *different* from other markets.

SELL A YARD OF CABLE

I was the treasurer of the New York branch of a Swiss bank in the late 1980s. We had a client who was a cotton merchant from Turkey. He speculated in forex as a paying hobby. Late one afternoon in New York, he called one of our dealers and placed an order to sell a "yard of cable." Let me translate that into English. What he wanted to do was to sell 1 billion British Pounds. (The only currency that is capitalized is the Pound; all others are lowercase. Forex trivia!) We were shocked at the size of the order. That would be a huge order for any major financial institution, let alone for a single individual. We were the counterparty on all orders from our customers so we were expected to take the other side of his trade. No way. We weren't big enough to take on such a large position.

All foreign exchange trading, except for a small amount on the International Monetary Market, is over the counter. There is no exchange. All transactions are done over the phone, with a broker, or via some electronic means between two entities. Entities are usually financial institutions but are often corporations and sometimes individuals. That means that when a retail investor, such as myself, puts in an order through an online broker, the counterparty is practically unknown. It could very well be the broker. However, the broker could be aggregating prices from different brokers or institutions. The source of the prices are unknown, which is very different from the stock market because a stock is generally traded only at one place, such as the New York Stock Exchange (NYSE). Technically, the NASDAQ is an over-the-counter market that is centralized in one place so it is, effectively, an exchange. Forex is completely diversified.

Back to the yard of cable. The size of his order meant that we had to lay off the risk to other dealers. But there was no way that we could find a dealer to take the whole billion Pounds. Even 100 million Pounds was a large order.

It was very late in the afternoon and I only had a few forex dealers on the desk. My main trading desk was in the form of a large T with me at the top of the T. I could see and hear everything on the desk this way. I started grabbing dealers from other desks. It took a few minutes but I soon assembled a cast of ten forex, bond, and cash dealers arrayed in front of me, five on each side of the bottom of the T.

We knew that the pressure of selling 1 million cable was going to cause a sharp drop in the price of the Pound Sterling. It was a huge order. So, naturally, we sold $20 million for our own account. It didn't change the price at all. This is called *front running* and is legal in forex and bond trading but illegal in stock trading. I told each trader to call a different bank and get a price for 100 million Pounds. In the interbank world, you ask for a price from the other bank. The other bank must offer you a two-sided market.

This means that they must give you a quoted price for both buying and selling. So the other dealers might have said "43–45," which means that they are willing to buy Pounds at 43 and to sell them at 45. Notice that 43 and 45 are not complete prices. The complete price might have been 1.6543 and 1.6545. But dealers only speak about the last two figures of the price. It is assumed that we all know the "handle" or the "big fig(ure)." Dealers don't waste time. In fact, the price of 43–45 was likely barked into the phone with the implication that we better quickly tell them whether we were buyers or sellers. I would often hear dealers say something like "43 45, whaddya want?" Their quote is two-sided (both a bid and an ask) and is a push to trade.

I told my dealers to raise their hand when they had a price. I gave them the sign to sell as soon as I saw my tenth dealer raise his hand. They all simultaneously said, "Yours, 100." Saying "yours" meant that the Pounds were sold to the buyer and were theirs. We would have said "mine" if we were buyers. The "100" was the quantity that we sold them, in this case, 100 million Pounds.

We were able to sell all billion Pounds that our client wanted us to sell. We sold them all at the current market price. But then all hell broke loose.

The pressure from our order caused a vacuum to open up under the price. We may have sold a billion cable at 43 but the price was 100 pips lower in a fraction of the second. A *pip* is the smallest normal increment that a currency trades in even though some brokers quote in tenths of a pip. A general rule of thumb is to start with the far-left digit in a price and count to the right five places and that is a pip. The yen under 100.00 is an exception. In that case, only count four places. Always ignore decimal places.

Our phone board lit up like Times Square. All ten of those dealers we had just sold to were screaming into the phone some variation of how we had stuffed them and how our parentage was suspect. They were screaming about how they were now holding a big position in Pounds and had nowhere to lay off the risk since we had basically forced the market to go long. They now owned 1 billion cable and had no one to lay off the risk to since we had just swamped the market. We let the other dealers vent for a minute or two and then explained that we had no choice in how we handled the order. They all stopped venting and agreed that they would have done exactly the same thing and there were no hard feelings. Indeed, we found ourselves on the other side of such a trade over and over again. This is financial Darwin in action. Now, remember, we sold short 20 million Pounds before we stuffed the market. We had a huge profit in that position now. I remember one of my traders saying to me that we just had a good year in the last minute. Yes, we made a lot of money on that trade. It was now time to mend some bridges. We could take that 20 million cable and go into the market and buy it back, thus taking our profits on the short position. We would dole out our 20 million to the dealers that had complained the least to reward their attitude. We couldn't offer a lot of relief but we were the only bidders in the market at that point so they were very happy to hear from us. On this trade, we were not trying to get the best price. With the client's order, we really wanted to get the best price. But for ourselves, we wanted to get out at a reasonable price and, at the same time, give back a little love to the market after we had decimated it.

In this case, we called a few brokers and, after letting them rant a little more, told them that we were buyers of cable. That was a signal to them that they could move the price up a pip or two and make a little money on our order.

Did I mention that trading forex is the most cutthroat of all the major markets to trade in?

DON'T WANT TO TRADE!

I've always considered it one of my greatest trading feats that Deutsche Bank never traded with me. The Deutsche mark was still being traded when I was a dealer. The euro came later. Deutsche Bank was the premier bank trading the mark. They were the big dog in the mark and really made the market for the mark. They had all the big clients so they saw most of the flow into the market. I mentioned before that we would generally quote a market with both sides. If we quoted a price of 65–67, that meant that we would sell it to whoever called us for a price at 67 and buy it from them at 65. So, for example, another dealer would call me and say, "Price on mark." That's all. That meant that they wanted a price for me to both buy or sell the D-mark. They don't tell me in which direction they want to go. They could be buyers or sellers. This process keeps the system fair. I have to give them a fair price since I don't know what they want to do. Otherwise, consider if I knew that they wanted to be buyers. I could then shade the price a little higher so they would have to bid up to my price to buy. That way, I would make a little more money. The two-sided quote keeps the market fair and also keeps the dealers on the ball.

The same situation applies to the online forex world. Two prices are always on the screen. The lower price is the bid and is the price that we will get when we sell a contract of forex. The higher price is the ask, or offer and is the price you will pay when you buy a contract of forex. I was always very afraid when Deutsche Bank would call me looking for a price on the mark. They were the largest dealer in the currency. They knew what the price was and had a huge inventory of marks. The only reason they would call me was to try to pick me off. They wanted to see if I was quoting the price of the mark correctly. If I was on the money, they would simply say, "Nothing there," and hang up the phone. However, they would do a trade with me if I was quoting the price incorrectly. For example, let's say that the market was 63–65. But they would sell to me if I quoted them 64–66. They would sell to me at 64 knowing that they could buy at 63 from their clients, thus making a pip on the trade. I was always very proud of the fact that they would always say "nothing there" whenever they would call me. That meant that I had quoted the market correctly. I would have most certainly lost money if they had done a trade with me. They knew that market far better than I did.

There are a lot of different currencies in the world to trade but the volume is concentrated in just a few. The most popular are (with nickname and official name):

- Euro versus dollar (euro; EUR/USD)
- Dollar versus yen (yen; USD/JPY)
- British Pound versus dollar (Pound, cable, or Sterling; GBP/USD)
- Dollar versus Swiss franc (Swissy; USD/CHF)
- Dollar versus Canadian dollar (Loonie or Canuck Buck; CAD/USD)
- Dollar versus Australian dollar (Oz or Aussie; AUD/USD)
- Euro versus yen (EUR/JPY)
- Euro versus Pound (EUR/GBP)
- Euro versus Swiss franc (EUR/CHF)

You'll notice that every currency is a pair. You are always long one side of the pair versus being short the other side of the pair. You can be long or short either side. When you buy EUR/USD, you are actually buying the euro while simultaneously selling short the dollar. When you short the EUR/USD, you are actually selling short the euro while simultaneously buying the dollar. That is the convention.

Let's take a look at the Swissy or the USD/CHF as an example. First, what does *CHF* stand for? It stands for Confederation Helvetia franc. They don't call it Switzerland in Switzerland, they call the country Helvetia. The currency unit is called the Swissy even though the pair starts out with a USD. The Swissy is the USD/CHF. Foreign exchange in the interbank world is usually traded in units of a million dollars. The typical trade is for $5 million. The normal futures contract calls for delivery of 125,000 of whatever is being traded. So the Swiss franc contract calls for delivery of 125,000 Swiss francs. The retail forex world has a standard contract worth $100,000 of whatever is being traded. So trading the euro would mean that you would be trading $100,000 worth of euros. Of course, the number of euros that you would be trading would change based on the current price of the euro. There are now mini-contracts in the online forex world where each contract is worth $10,000 of the underlying instrument. In fact, there are now micro-contracts of $1,000 of the underlying instrument. The usual minimum unit that a pair can trade is called a *pip*. You can find out the value of a pip by multiplying the pip by the contract size that you are trading. For example, suppose that you are trading a standard online contract of euro. That would be $100,000 worth of euro. The euro is quoted like 1.5123. One figure to the left of the decimal place and four to the right (although there are now online brokers who quote in tenths of pips). So take the rule of thumb that the pip is the fifth figure from the left (the exception being yen when it is quoted under 100.00). The value of a pip for a standard online contract would be 0.0001 times $100,000, or $10. The value of a pip actually changes during the day as the value of the underlying instrument changes. In addition, some brokers may change the contract size less often. It is always best to double-check with each broker. In the futures world, pips are called *ticks* and are always worth $12.50. This is because the futures contracts are standardized at 125,000 francs, euros, or whatever. The only exception is the Pound, for which the contract is 62,500 Pounds and each tick is worth $6.25. The standard unit of trading in the interbank market is $5 million while in the retail forex market it is only $100,000. Does this mean that banks must come up with $5 million and we have to come up with $100,000 every time we want to do a trade? Thankfully, no. There is no margin or good-faith deposit in the interbank market. Instead, banks do deals with each other simply on credit. A bank will have its credit officers examine the credit of the other potential trading banks. The credit officer might say that the forex department can have a total exposure of up to $100 million. The forex desk could then do one big deal worth $100 million or perhaps ten different deals of $10 million each. The total, however, can't be over $100 million. The risk in the forex world is not strictly a credit risk since there is no credit being extended. There is just a delivery risk.

Consider this scenario: We have just bought 5 million euro/yen from Widget Bank, which means that we must deliver 5 million euro worth of yen to them and they must deliver 5 million euro to us. The risk in this transaction is called *delivery risk* because the other side of the trade may fail to deliver, in this case 5 million euro. Forex trades are settled within one day so the delivery risk is a one-day risk. But let's say that we are in that trade for 10 days. In the interbank world, the initial trade gets rolled over every day as if it were a new trade. The delivery risk is eliminated from the previous day but the very same delivery risk comes into play until the very last day when everything is reversed and there is no risk. It is very different in the online forex and futures worlds. Here, we must post a margin deposit every time we do a trade. Although it is termed *margin*, it is different from margin in the stock world. In stocks, margin is a form of lending that uses stock as collateral. Interest must be paid on the balance owed to the broker. Margin in the forex world is simply a good-faith deposit. You can even sometimes earn interest on it. The broker will freeze a certain amount of money for each contract you enter into. They will not allow you to put on a trade if there is not enough margin in the account. For example, the margin to enter a long EUR/USD trade in our online trading account is $500 for a standard contract. We have $1,000 in our account. The broker will allow us to enter no more than two contracts. However, we have to have that $1,000 margin for those two accounts at all times. If the position starts to lose money, the broker has the right to liquidate the position. They do that to make sure that you always have enough money in your account in case a position goes against you. And, yes, they will liquidate your open positions in an instant if you go below the margin position in your account. The situation is similar in futures.

TRANSACTION COSTS

The biggest transaction cost in trading forex is the bid/ask spread. The *bid/ask spread* is the difference between the bid price and the ask, or offer, price. For example, suppose that the market is 63 bid and 66 offered or asked. You will have to buy at 66 if you want to buy or sell at 63 if you want to sell. Let's assume that you buy at 66. For the interbank and futures trader, the price on the screen will show 66 and it will appear that you have a break-even trade. However, if you were to instantaneously try to sell it, you would sell it at 63 for a three-pip loss. Online brokers will immediately show that you have a three-pip loss because they will show the bid price as the last price not the last price. No matter how it is presented, you will have an instant loss of three pips when you enter a trade with a three-pip spread. Hopefully the market will move in your direction right away and eliminate that bid/ask spread loss. But, obviously, it can also go the other direction. The point is that the bid/ask is an implicit cost in every transaction. The bid/ask spread can be anywhere from one pip to tens of pips.

The more liquid the instrument, the narrower or tighter the bid/ask spread. So, generally, it is much cheaper to trade EUR/USD than GBP/AUD. The bid/ask could be ten pips on the GBP/AUD at the same time the EUR/USD may only be two pips. Everybody pays the bid/ask spread unless you are a dealer, which essentially means that you are a large bank. In the case of the large bank dealers, they are the ones who are making the bid/ask spread and that is a major profit center for the banks. They quote the bid/ask spread to the online brokers and implicitly into the futures market. They are willing to sell to us at the ask and willing to buy from us for the bid. They implicitly make that bid/ask spread as a profit. That compensates them for providing us with the ability to trade whenever we want to. Futures traders and sometimes interbank players must pay a commission. Futures traders must always pay a commission to their broker to execute their trade. Interbank traders will sometimes execute a trade through an interbank broker and will have to pay a pip or a half pip to the broker to execute that trade.

Transaction costs become more important the shorter the time horizon of the trader. A person who is going to hold a position for months could care less about the cost of the bid/ask spread. A three-pip spread over months is irrelevant. But three pips is highly important for a trader who is doing many trades throughout the day. Their profit objective may only be 20 pips; three pips is a significant hit on profitability. Remember, the trader has to implicitly pay the three pips when you both enter and exit a trade. Effectively, the day trader is paying six pips to make 20.

IT NEVER STOPS

Technically, forex trading begins Sunday morning in Tel Aviv and goes to Friday afternoon in New York. However, the Tel Aviv session is so small that it is usually ignored and trading starts on Monday morning in Wellington, New Zealand.

Traditionally, the trading day begins in Wellington because it is the first trading center that opens. However, Wellington is a small trading center so there is little trading. Trading really becomes more active when Sydney and Tokyo open. The London forex center is the center with the highest volume, so trading really takes off when it opens. New York opens when London is at lunch and is the center with the second-highest volume of trading. The period with the highest volume is during the afternoon in London and the morning of New York. London then closes, leaving New York as the final trading center open for the day. There is decent volume in the New York afternoon except, perhaps, on Friday afternoon. The slowest time of the day is between the time New York closes and Wellington opens.

The cycle never ends.

MY BIGGEST LOSING TRADE

There are three main orders you can place in the forex market though online brokers can be more creative. The first order is the *market order*. In this case, the order could be to "buy 5 at market" or "sell 8 at market."

The quantity changes with each order. As mentioned earlier, the market always has a bid price and an ask, or offer, price. A market order to buy is always filled at the ask and a market order to sell is always filled at the bid. The only exception is when the quantity to buy or sell is larger than the quantity on the bid or ask. For example, you want to sell eight contracts at the market. The bid is 79 but there are only five bids at that price. There are three bids just below that at 78. So you would sell five at 79 and three at 78. A market order must be filled by the broker at the best bid or ask immediately.

A *limit order* is an order to buy when the market goes lower or to sell the market when it rallies. Let's assume that the market is 38 bid and 39 ask. A limit order would be to buy the pair when it dips to a level below the current market. So, for example, you would put in an order to buy two contracts at 33 limit. Your order will be filled when the market trades or is offered at 33. You will use the limit order whenever you want to buy a dip in the market or sell a rally.

The stop order is the order I use more than any other. A *stop order* is used when you want to buy something at a price *higher* than the current market or wish to sell a pair at a price *below* the current market price. Consider this: The market is 38 bid and 39 ask. A stop order would be used to buy the pair when it rallies up to 45. So, for example, an order to buy two contracts at 45 stop would be placed. It becomes a market order when the market trades or is bid at 45. The order will be filled at whatever the best offer is at that time.

Use a stop order when you want to buy a pair at a price higher than the current price. A stop order is often called a *stop loss order* because the most common use of a stop order is to exit a position. For example, a limit order can be used to buy EUR/USD at 135.60. To exit the trade, you should it trade down to 135.30. You would enter an order to sell at 125.30 stop. This would become a market order to sell if the market trades or is offered at 135.30. However, I use stop orders almost exclusively. A lot of people think I'm crazy because they don't understand why I would want to pay a high price for something using a stop order instead of a lower price using a limit price. Buy low, sell high, they say to me.

The first problem with limit orders is that you almost always have a losing trade immediately. For example, you have an order to buy a pair at 85 limit. You can only be filled if the market trades at 85 or is offered at 85. In the real world, the price will drop below the 85 limit price in order to get filled. The next pip after you have been filled will be 84 and, most likely, the price will move even lower before finding support. That means that you will be sitting on a losing trade right away. The more important problem with limit orders is that they break one of the basic tenets of profitable forex trading: *Don't fight the market.* Buying using a limit order is buying when the market is dropping. You don't want to buy when the market is dropping. The market is telling you that the situation is bearish because it is dropping in price. I never want to go against the market. It is bigger, faster, smarter, and better looking than I am. We will always lose the battle if we fight the market.

Entering on a stop order creates a very different dynamic. You are nearly always in a profit position immediately. After all, you can be filled on a stop order until the market is trading at or higher than your stop order. The short-term momentum of the market will nearly always push the price beyond your entry price by at least a little bit. I'll take that profit edge any day. More important, using entry stop orders ensures that we are in tune with the market. We are only buying when the market is bullish and only selling when the market is bearish. This means that we have the wind to our back, not to our face. We are in sync with the market and, therefore, have the power of the market behind us. It may not stay there long but it is always better to at least be in tune with the market for at least the beginning of any trade.

The only time to use limit orders is when there is a liquidity problem with buying on a stop. I would have to use limit orders to buy when I traded for institutions because the size of my stop order would cause the market to go sky high. I need to be buying when others are selling, or else selling when others are buying so that I wouldn't affect the market. Fortunately, we retail traders don't have to worry about this.

I was heading up a derivatives trading desk in the late 1980s. One of the derivatives we dealt and traded was options on forex. We had a book of derivatives and then used a large quantity of forex to hedge the risk. There was a big economic release coming up that day. I was using forex futures to hedge my position. In particular, I was short the Swiss franc in large quantity and other currencies in lesser quantities. I was short hundreds of contracts. Bingo! The number was released and the market skyrocketed. I ended up having my protective stop filled about 150 ticks or pips above where my stop had been placed! There was a complete vacuum of orders above the market. The brokers couldn't fill my orders until 150 pips above my stop.

The other interesting thing is that the cash market peaked about 100 pips under the futures market. In other words, there was much more liquidity in the cash market than in the futures market. I got hammered. I lost about $450,000 in less than 10 seconds. I should have lost about $150,000 because I had the wrong trade but the incredibly bad fill cost me another $300,000. It seemed like the longest walk in my life as I trudged through the trading room to report my loss to my boss, the treasurer of the bank. In this case, the price jumped over the stop order leaving me with a fill 100 pips beyond the stop order. That can happen with stop orders. That was a rare circumstance, but it can happen. It is fairly common to have a stop order filled a pip or two away from the stop level in your order. Just get used to it. I actually don't mind getting filled a little off my price because it shows that the market is moving so powerfully that there is a shortage of orders on the other side of my trade. I like that imbalance. I don't like it when I get a bad fill on a protective stop order. I want to get out at my price when I use a stop to protect an open position. On the other hand, I feel fortunate to get out, even with a bad fill, when the market gaps down beyond my stop because that means that there is so much pressure that there is no buying in the market. I definitely don't want to be long in that kind of a market!

Note that this kind of situation never occurs with a limit order. You will always be filled at your limit price. Of course, you may be in deep trouble if that happens. Let's say you want to buy at 50 when the market is at 60. A big news item comes out and the market drops precipitously. You will be filled at 50 but the next print of the price may not be until 30. Basically, you were filled at a price that was way above the market. A market order will always be filled when the market is moving dramatically. However, it may be far away from the price on the screen when you entered the order and you may be left chasing the market to get filled.

THE BOTTOM LINE

Knowing the nitty-gritty of forex trading is important when you want to make money in the market (which is always!). Learn how to enter orders correctly and enhance your profits through understanding which orders will optimize your order.

CHAPTER 2

Trend Analysis

The Basis for All
Technical Analysis

I n the late 1980s, I used to trade a lot of mechanical technical systems. I had fundamental regression models of just about every market you could think of. I worked all day just feeding my computer with data and then putting in orders based on the output.

But I had an epiphany.

Why was I working so hard? I went through all my systems and realized that many of them were so highly correlated that there was no point to them.

I also applied the Pareto Principle, which states that 80 percent of the profits will come from 20 percent of the methods. And, in fact, that was basically the truth. I could cut out 80 percent of my work but still make 80 percent of the profits.

In the mid-1990s I had the opportunity to interview Peter Brandt. Peter was running a futures newsletter called *The Factor*, which was using strict Magee/Edwards chart analysis. He was a purist in using classical chart analysis. One of the things he said to me was that there are only about eight to twelve mega markets in the futures world each year. By *mega market*, he meant a market that created at least $5,000 in profit and usually much more. That $5,000 in profit was the amount of money that would be made by holding a position for the length of the total move. I looked at futures charts going back many years and he was basically right.

He then went on to say that his job as a position trader was to capture only those mega moves. His ideal trading year was if he caught only those trades. He felt the ideal year would only have eight to twelve trades. Every other trade was not worth the risk.

That might be an extreme view but there is some truth to his concept. So I decided to strip my trading down to the bare essentials. I wanted to really get to the heart of trading. No BS, just rock-bottom truth. In fact, I wanted to strip things down so low that what I would come up with would sound like child's play.

The basic truth of trading is that we must be long when the market is bullish, be short when it is bearish, and stand aside when it is neutral. Simple, yes?

Let me say it again. Be long when bullish, be short when bearish, and stand aside the rest of the time.

Easy to say, but is it easy to do? Yes!

WHAT IS A TREND?

Turns out that there is a classic definition of a bull or bear market. A *bull market* is any market that is making higher highs and higher lows. A *bear market* is any market that is making lower highs and lower lows. A *neutral market* is any other condition. Once again, this is very simple.

However, it is simple only if we agree on what a high or low is. And that has traditionally been a subjective decision. First, let's make a definition. The highs and lows that we are looking for will be called *swing highs* and *swing lows*. That will clear up some confusion with the highs and lows on each daily bar. Let's take a look at a chart and see where the swing highs and swing lows are (see Figure 2.1).

I've circled a number of swing highs and lows on this chart during the period August through November. In this chart, you and I likely agreed on where the swing highs and lows were. We intuitively agreed. We didn't have a rule that said what constituted a high or low because, as humans, we can intuitively agree.

But what if we disagree? What if you pick one high and I don't agree? What about the high five bars before the end of August? We skipped over those because we agreed that they were not important or significant. So the real key is to understand which swing highs are significant. We intuitively skipped over the insignificant highs and lows. But there may come a time when we may disagree on the significance of a given high or low. It would be better to have an objective way to determine the significance.

My friend Tom DeMark is perhaps the most innovative technical analyst in history. He has probably added more and better technical indicators than anyone in history. One of his innovations is the idea of creating objective standards for what was traditionally considered subjective. For example, how do you label Elliott Waves? More germane to this discussion:

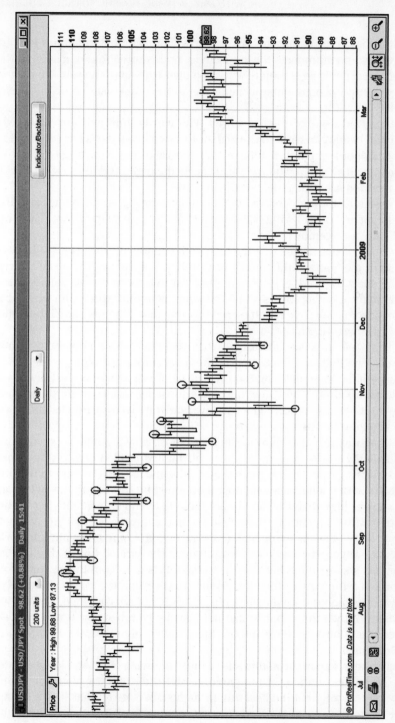

FIGURE 2.1 Japanese Yen with Highs and Lows Circled

What highs should be used to create a downward sloping trendline? His objective criteria eliminates the subjectivity that is often found in such types of technical analysis as Elliott Wave and classical chart analysis. No longer will you and I disagree about the proper slope of a trendline or the Wave count.

First, let me clarify some terms. The words *high* and *low* have two meanings. They can refer to the high or low of a given day's bar (or candle) or the high or low point of a move over several or more days. Let's call this last meaning swing high and swing low. So the highs and lows on the chart that I circled are swing high and swing lows.

Basically, DeMark showed that certain swing highs and swing lows are significant and other swing highs and swing lows are insignificant. The way he did it was ingenious.

I think we can agree that the high in the middle of April is more important than the highs in the middle of October. We can see that very clearly on the chart. DeMark created a method for determining how significant a swing high or swing low is. (The following is my interpretation of what I learned from him. Give him the credit for the initial genius and I'll take the blame for screwing it up!)

The basic idea is to identify every swing high with an objective rating system. The high in mid-August is the most important high on the chart because it is the highest high on the chart. The lows made in December and January are the two most important lows because they are the lowest lows on the chart. Major highs and lows show up as major highs and lows because they are the most extreme.

DeMark's rating system is simple. Choose a swing high or swing low in Figure 2.1. For example, let's look at the first circled high on the chart from August. Now, look at the bar after this one and all the bars to the left of it. To be defined as a swing high there must be one bar to the right that has a lower high than the day we are looking at and at least one bar to the left of it with a high lower than the high on the day we are looking at. That simple test defines a swing high (reverse everything for a swing low). We have objectively defined every swing high. The circled bar at the high in August is a swing high but the bar to the left is not. Note that it has a bar to the left with a lower high but the bar to the right, the circled bar, has a high that is higher than the bar's high. So it is not a swing high. The bar to the right of the circled bar is also not a swing high because it has a lower bar to the right but the circled bar has a higher high than the bar that we are looking at.

The next step in the analysis is to rank the swing highs and lows. We do this by simply counting the number of bars to the left of the bar in question. Let's do this with the highest bar in August. We know that it is a swing high because it has at least one bar on either side of it with a lower high.

However, there are 41 bars to the left of it with a high on the bar that is lower than the high on the circled bar. I would call that a 41-bar swing high because there are 41 lower highs to the left of it. There might be even more than that but we got to the edge of the chart.

Let's now look at the next circled bar to the right of the one we just looked at in Figure 2.1. That would be a low four days after that major 41-bar high. Once again, let's count bars. We know that there is one to the right and 10 bars to the left before we run into a bar that has a lower low. I'd call that a 10-bar low.

You can go through all the highs and lows on the whole chart rating them by how many bars they have to the left. It is clear that we intuitively rank bars with higher numbers as being more significant than bars with fewer numbers. This then leads to the concept that we can now use objectivity when describing chart patterns. For example, we can now agree that we will only draw up trendlines that connect five bar or higher lows. Looking at the chart, identify all the five-bar lows and draw a trendline connecting the two most recent five-bar lows. We will never disagree about where to draw the trendline because we have agreed that five-bar lows are significant.

Which leads to the next step in our journey. What bar level is significant? What bar level should we be focusing on to eliminate little random blip movements and keep us focused on what is really important?

My experience is that three-bar highs and lows are significant and that two- and one-bar highs and lows are not. Of course, there can be exceptions but that is a strong general rule. Markets can often retrace against the trend for a day or two but rarely will they move three days without it meaning something.

To check this, look back at Figure 2.1 and look for three-bar highs and lows for trend analysis. I find that this bar level keeps me in the trend and avoids getting stopped out on random little blips.

Let me digress for one moment. Every technique I teach has a stop loss attached to it. Most techniques taught in other books have stops attached to them. For me, I want every stop loss technique to have two attributes.

First, the stop should only be triggered when something significant happens. I don't want to be stopped out on some little squirrelly move in the market. Or perhaps just one big trade moves the market. I only want to exit a trade on a significant move.

Second, I only want to be stopped out when I know that I am wrong. As long as there is no evidence that my original thesis is wrong, I must stay with the trade. I'll let a trade go against me a little when that movement is insignificant and does not invalidate my original trade idea.

The ranking of swing highs and lows allows us to measure how significant a move is, thereby satisfying condition number one. We will not be stopped out on trivial moves but only moves that have some power be-hind them. Later in the chapter, I'll show you how this ranking allows us to satisfy condition number two.

From now on, I'm going to focus only on significant swing highs and lows, previously defined as three-bar highs or lows. We're going to ignore all swing highs and lows that are two-bar highs or lows.

Let's take a look at Figure 2.2. This chart shows the same currency pair over basically the same time frame but I have changed the circles from what I intuitively identified as significant swing highs and lows to what I have now objectively defined as three-bar high and lows. Note that there are not too many changes. The chart is roughly the same. However, now the significant highs and lows are objectively defined. Using our agreed-upon definitions, our significant highs and lows would be the same.

HOW TO PROFITABLY TRADE BULL AND BEAR MARKETS

Now that we agree on what the trend is in the market, we can go to the next step. Remember that a bull market is defined as a market that is mak-ing higher highs and higher lows. A bear market is a market that is mak-ing lower highs and lower lows. A neutral market is defined as any other condition.

The highs and lows can come in any order. So, we could make two highs followed by two lows. Generally, however, we oscillate between highs and lows such that we make a high, a low, a high, and then a final low. But remember, it doesn't matter in what order the highs and lows occur.

At the top of the chart in Figure 2.3, look at the high in August. I've labeled the first four highs and lows. Note that in this case, the second high is lower than the first high; we can say that we are making lower highs. Also note that the second swing low is lower than the first low. Thus, we can say that we are making lower lows. This is the definition of a bear market.

My concept is very simple but powerful. We must always be long in bull markets, be short in bear markets, and stand aside in all other markets. This is the basis for the most profitable technical analysis.

We only need to look at the two most recent highs and two most recent lows to determine if it is a bull, bear, or neutral market. The analysis is updated every time a market makes a new significant swing high or low. That new swing high or low is added to our analysis. Usually, that new

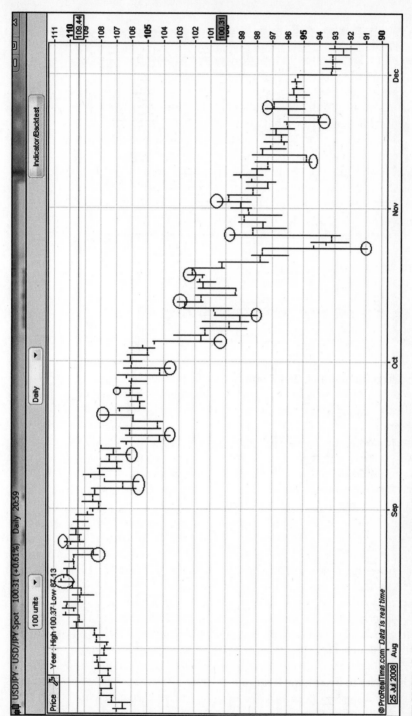

FIGURE 2.2 Japanese Yen with Highs and Lows Marked

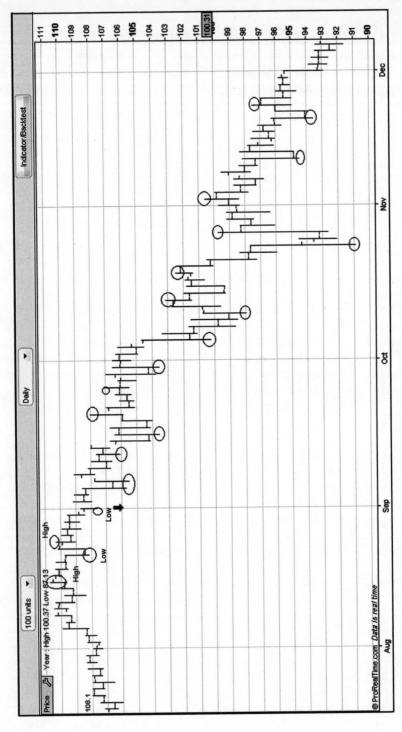

FIGURE 2.3 Japanese Yen with Highs and Lows Marked and First Four Labeled

high or low simply confirms the current analysis but sometimes it changes the trend.

The fifth circle on the chart is a lower low than the previous low, so it merely confirms what is already a bear market. But look at the sixth circle. It is a higher low. So, at that point in time, the market is making lower highs but higher lows. So, it's a neutral market, right? The market then breaks lower and the next circle is a new lower low and the bear market is back in place.

HOW TO TRADE THE TREND

Once you understand significant swing highs or lows, trading the markets becomes easy. Go long when the market turns into a bull market, go short when the market turns into a bear market, and stand aside when the market is in any other condition. Let's take a look at some examples.

In Figure 2.4, start at the top swing high in August. That is our first swing high. It is then followed by a swing low and then a swing high. Note that I have drawn a horizontal line at the low of the first swing low. Our rule is to go short when the market breaks that horizontal line at the low of the first swing low. I've put an arrow pointing down on the day that we go short. We go short the moment the market drops below the low of the first swing low. I don't have to wait until the second swing low is in place to go short. Note that I am getting short before the second swing low is in place because I know that we will definitely be putting in a lower low in the future. I don't know when, but it will happen. There is no possible way that we won't put in a new lower swing low after we break that first low. In this case, the lower low that confirms that we are in a bear market actually occurs on the day the market breaks down through the first swing low.

In other words, I can put in a sell short order under the first swing low as soon as I have a confirmed lower high. At the second high, I have conformed half of the definition of a bear market: lower highs. Now all I need to get short is to wait for a break of the first swing low to confirm that we will be making a lower low, again confirming a bear market. Once again, I don't need to wait until the lower low occurs to get short. I just need to know that it will be coming. And that knowledge comes as soon as I break the first swing low.

The stop on short positions is the most recent three-bar high. The protective stop on long positions is always the most recent significant swing low. I get to move the stop up whenever I am long and we make a new higher low. I get to move the stop down whenever I am short and we make a new lower high.

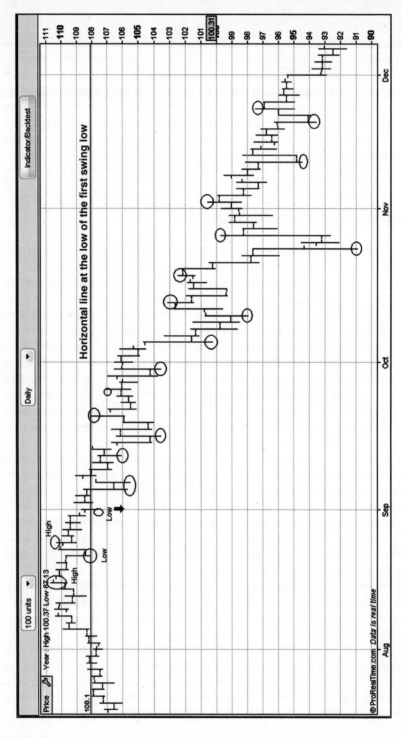

FIGURE 2.4 Japanese Yen with Breakdown

So, in this case, we go short on a break of the first swing low and place a protective stop loss just above the most recent swing high, which, in this case, is the second high on the chart.

The market then sells off and we are off to a good start on our short position. However, the fourth swing low turns out to be a higher low as you can see in Figure 2.5. I've marked it as a higher low.

Now, we didn't know that low was a higher low until the close of the next day. We need to see that extra day to let us know that day was a swing low. So we now see at the end of the day after the swing low that the swing low was, indeed, a swing low! We look back at the two most recent highs and see that the market is still making lower highs but we are now making higher lows. That is one of the definitions of a neutral market and our rule is that we must be on the sidelines whenever there is a neutral market. We exit the position on the open the next day for a modest profit.

We are now flat on the open of the day after the day after the swing low. We now look at the chart and notice that a break to below the most recent swing low would turn the market bearish. We put in a sell order to sell on a break of the most recent swing low. This move occurs later that day and is marked in the chart with a downward pointing arrow. We don't know when we will make a new swing low but we do know that it is guaranteed to occur so we go short. Our protective stop on this trade is way above the current market at the most recent swing high, which is the second high on the chart and was also our protective stop on the first trade. Remember, we don't need to actually see a lower low; we just have to know that one is guaranteed to come. And that guarantee comes when we break the most recent swing low.

We then make a lower swing low the following day and a lower swing high four days after getting short. We now get to lower our protective stop to just above the new lower swing high. Four days later, we make an even lower swing high so we lower our protective stop to just above that level.

The market then collapses, putting us into a nice profit position. Notice that we don't lower our stop at all until we finally make a lower high in mid-October. We go over two weeks with the old stop.

This is one of the interesting features that you will have to deal with as a trader. Remember that we want all stops to fulfill two conditions. First, we don't get stopped out on some random move and, second, we don't want to exit a position until after we know we are wrong. Trend analysis often gives the trader lots of room to work so that he or she is only stopped out when those two conditions are in place.

It can be psychologically difficult to watch a market drop dramatically, producing a big profit, yet the stop is not moved closer in the hopes that a bigger profit is to come. It is better to sometimes sit back and let the market

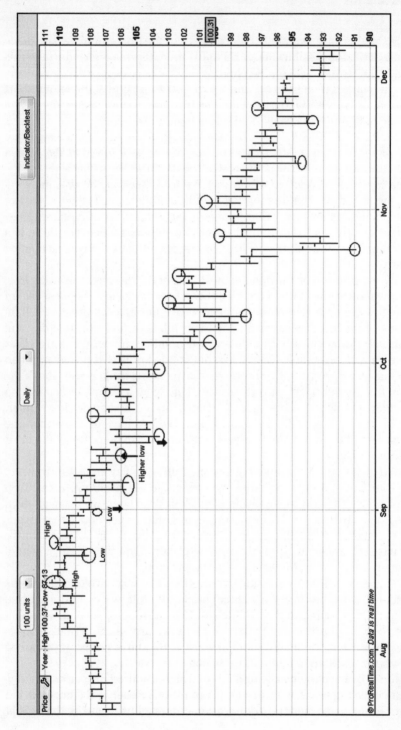

FIGURE 2.5 Japanese Yen with Second Breakdown

run. Here's what legendary trader Jesse Livermore said in *Reminiscences of a Stock Operator* (John Wiley & Sons, Inc., 1994):

> *And right here let me say one thing: After spending many years in Wall Street and after making and losing millions of dollars I want to tell you this: It never was my thinking that made the big money for me. It always was my sitting. Got that? My sitting tight! It is no trick at all to be right on the market. You always find lots of early bulls in bull markets and early bears in bear markets. I've known many men who were right at exactly the right time, and began buying and selling stocks when prices were at the very level which should show the greatest profit. And their experience invariably matched mine—that is, they made no real money out of it. Men who can both be right and sit tight are uncommon. I found it one of the hardest things to learn. But it is only after a stock operator has firmly grasped this that he can make big money. It is literally true that millions come easier to a trader after he knows how to trade than hundreds did in the days of his ignorance.*

That's right: Sitting is how he made his money. The point here is that traders should stick with positions that are making money. Don't exit them prematurely. I'll talk more about this in a later chapter.

Going back to Figure 2.5, we see that the market continues to drop off a cliff to the circled swing low seen in late October. Two sharp up days create a new lower swing high and we get to lower our protective stop to that new swing high. We then get stopped out for a significant profit five days later.

This sequence of swing highs and lows and the resulting trades gives you a clear idea of how to trade the trend in the market. It is technical analysis stripped down to the absolute essentials.

Let me repeat the rules. Go long the moment the market moves into a pattern of higher highs and higher lows. Note that all four points don't have to exist to get long but three of them do have to exist and the fourth must be in the process of being formed. The reverse is true for bearish markets.

MEGAPHONES AND PENNANTS

There are two neutral market formations to look out for: megaphones and pennants. You want to be looking out for them because it is harder to see entry points when the market is in a neutral phase than when it is in a bull or bear phase. Also, it will save you time if you can identify a megaphone formation because there is no entry possible with this formation while it is very likely that you will be filled soon on entering the market when there is a pennant formation.

A *megaphone formation* occurs when the market is making higher highs but lower lows. As a result, it looks like a megaphone if you draw a line connecting the highs and a line connecting the lows. Okay, it may look like a funny-shaped megaphone but you get the idea.

Take a look at the first swing high in November, shown in Figure 2.5. We have just put in a new swing high that is higher than the previous swing high of a week earlier. Note that the two most recent swing lows are forming lower lows. In sum, we are making higher highs and lower lows and thus forming a megaphone formation. This means that there is no possible way to enter the market. We can't be a buyer or a seller. We can't buy if we make a new high because it is still a neutral market because we are still making lower lows. We can't sell if we make a new low because it is still a neutral market because we are still making higher highs. Don't waste time looking at this pair if there is a megaphone formation because there is no way that you can get long or short. Go look at something else! Don't waste time here!

On the other hand, a *pennant formation* is an excellent sign that a new trade is imminent. You should be able to get long or short quickly. Let's look at an example. In Figure 2.5, start at the beginning of October and look to the left or back in time. Note that the two most recent highs are making lower highs. Note that the two most recent lows are making higher lows (the most recent low is just barely higher than the previous low).

In this case, we can put in two orders: (1) buy on a break of the most recent high, and (2) sell on a break down below the most recent low. It is likely that one of these two orders will be filled soon since a pennant formation is a formation where prices are winding up into a narrower and narrower range. It usually doesn't take long for the market to break out of the range and start to trend in one direction or the other.

A megaphone formation occurs when there is no direction in the market and a lot of volatility. I don't want to trade in a market like this. There is too much risk, due to the lack of direction yet high volatility.

A pennant formation occurs when the market comes into balance. Neither the bulls nor the bears have enough power to get the market to trend. That means that prices wind into a narrower and narrower range. At some point, either the bulls or the bears will gain enough strength to push the market out of the range and into a trend. We will be ready for this breakout no matter what direction it occurs. We will have orders to buy on a break of the most recent high and orders to sell on a break of the most recent low. Notice also that the stop on a pennant formation is likely to be fairly close to the market. Keep an eye out for pennant formations! You are about to make a trade!

AVERAGE DIRECTIONAL INDEX

I think that I have the greatest mentoring clients. I provide a mentoring service through the Investment Mentoring Institute. One of the great joys is that I get to learn a lot. My students are diligent about making money so they intensely investigate the markets. One of them came up with an improvement on what I was teaching and I want to share it with you.

First, let me tell you about average directional index (ADX). Here is how StockCharts.com (recommended for stock traders!) describes ADX:

> *J. Welles Wilder developed the Average Directional Index (ADX) to evaluate the strength of a current trend, be it up or down. It's important to determine whether the market is trending or trading (moving sideways), because certain indicators give more useful results depending on the market doing one or the other.*
>
> *The ADX is an oscillator that fluctuates between 0 and 100. Even though the scale is from 0 to 100, readings above 60 are relatively rare. Low readings, below 20, indicate a weak trend and high readings, above 40, indicate a strong trend. The indicator does not grade the trend as bullish or bearish, but merely assesses the strength of the current trend. A reading above 40 can indicate a strong downtrend as well as a strong uptrend.*
>
> *ADX can also be used to identify potential changes in a market from trending to non-trending. When ADX begins to strengthen from below 20 and moves above 20, it is a sign that the trading range is ending and a trend is developing.*[1]

J. Welles Wilder constructed ADX as an indicator that measured how strong a trend was no matter if it was up or down. The idea was not to identify the trend but the strength of whatever trend was in place. I won't go into how the index is constructed because there is plenty of information on the Internet.

I've tried many ways to use ADX but virtually everything didn't work. All of the commonly explained ways to use it aren't successful. So here are the two ways that you *can use* ADX to enhance your profitability.

ADX Filters

This is the method my student shared with me. I was going along teaching trend analysis and channel breakouts (discussed in Chapter 3) and my

---

[1]http://stockcharts.com/school/doku.php?id=chart_school:technical_indicators: average_directional

student used ADX as a filter for the trades I was teaching him. He used ADX to identify which trend analysis and channel breakout trades to take and which ones to leave alone. Guess what? His filter improved the performance of the basic techniques.

Stop and think about it. Trend analysis is a trend-following technique. We will make the most amount of money when the trends are strong and even lose money when the market is not trending.

The filter takes trend analysis trades *only* when the ADX is higher than it was the prior day. Don't take the signal if the ADX is lower than the day before. It's that simple. What this does is to take out any trades that may occur while the market is not trending. A declining ADX means that the market is not trending so the filter is taking us out of trades when the market is not trending. Only getting into trades when the ADX is climbing means that we are getting into markets that are already trending in our direction. This increases the potential size of the winning trade while also reducing the chances of a losing trade.

This filter will sometimes eliminate a winning trade but it eliminates far more losing trades to create a net improvement to the bottom line.

THE BISHOP

The second way that I use ADX is for a technique I call the Bishop because it is almost infallible. This is an exit-only strategy. It is so simple that everyone always seems to make it more complicated than it is.

Take a look at Figure 2.6. Across the bottom you will see the ADX indicator. Actually, there are two lines on the chart but you should only look at the line that is more volatile. The other line is a smoothing of the first line.

I look for the ADX line to be above 40 and then turn down. I then exit my trend-following positions in all the techniques that I teach in this book, including trend analysis and channel breakouts.

I never look at the ADX if it is below 40. I exit my positions on the first down day, no matter how small a downtick, in the ADX. Let me repeat: I don't care about any other pattern or level. I only care that ADX is above 40 and ticks lower. I'm only concerned with the day of the downtick after being above 40. I don't care about the day after the day it turns down. Don't complicate this indicator! Keep it simple.

There is one Bishop signal on this chart. Notice the peak in the ADX near the end of October. The ADX is above 40 and then turns down one bar after the lowest bar on the chart. We would then exit all of our

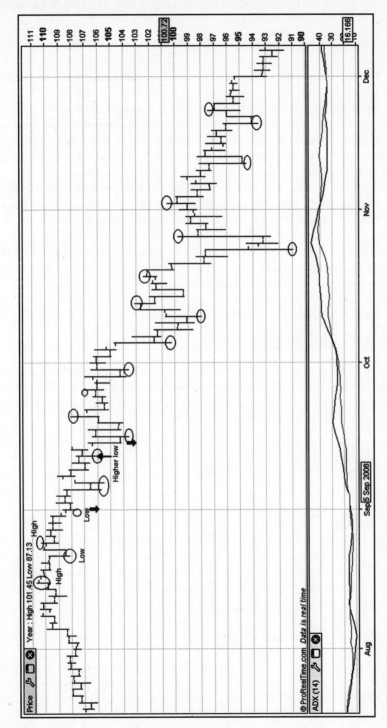

FIGURE 2.6 Japanese Yen with ADX Indicators

29

trend-following positions in trend analysis, channel breakout, and CoFlex and go flat.

This signal was a great signal at the time, as it got us out of the market the day after the low in the market at that time. We were able to take some great profits in the various method.

We don't get many Bishop signals but they tend to be great when we do. I find that about half of the signals are astounding and get me out at or near the end of a trend. The others get me out at a good time but I end up getting back in later.

One of the issues of trend following is that you generally have to give back a fair portion of the profits when you finally exit the position. Trend following is designed to get you to take out the middle of the move of a big trend.

The Bishop is a major enhancement of classic trend following because it allows you to take profits at or near the end of the trend in many cases. Not all cases but a good percentage of times.

THE BOTTOM LINE

Trend analysis is a solid profitable performer. It is a method that will get you into bull and bear markets of intermediate length. It guarantees that you will make money while the market is trending strongly but it will also enable you to profit from a short-term trend.

CHAPTER 3

Channel Breakouts

The Trend Is Your Friend

P robably more money has been made using channel breakout techniques in forex than with any other technique. This is a pretty strong statement. But you can look at the 10 largest CTAs or public forex trading companies and you will see that virtually every one of them is using some form of channel breakouts.

This incredible precept should make every trader stand up and pay *very* close attention; it should be a core technique for every forex trader.

THE BEGINNINGS OF CHANNEL BREAKOUTS

The first real description of channel breakouts came from investing pioneer Richard Donchian. Donchian was the creator of the first publicly traded futures fund, in 1948. He was an innovator in the field of technical analysis. His ideas form the basis for some of the most successful traders of all time. He was the person who first coined the term *trend following* and was one of the most important technical analysts of all time.

One of his most famous and successful ideas was his Four-Week Rule. He designed it for trading stocks and futures but the concept works for forex. The basic rules are incredibly simple to follow.

You buy the currency pair when it makes a new four-week high or sell when it makes a new four-week low. If you get long, then you reverse and go short if it makes a new four-week low. If you get short, then you reverse and go long if it makes a new four-week high. That's it! Simple!

Turns out that this simple system has been consistently profitable since he first wrote about it in the 1960s. However, there have been many enhancements by others to the basic rules outlined by Donchian.

There has been a lot of research into channel breakouts in the intervening years. Channel breakouts became perhaps the most dominant form of trend following in the 1980s. Famous traders, such as Richard Dennis, became incredibly rich and famous using channel breakouts. Now, billions of dollars are being traded using channel breakouts.

I think that the basic premise behind channel breakouts was that prices would drift sideways unless a new fundamental environment came into play. New fundamental data would cause the market to need to discount that new information and cause the price to move in one direction or another. This movement caused by a change in the fundamentals would trigger a buy or sell signal on the channel breakout. The channel breakout was not predicting a change in prices but was adept at identifying them.

Another way to look at it was to consider what must be happening in a market to cause the price to make a new one-month high. Something, we don't know what, must be happening that is significant in order to cause the price to move to a new one-month high. Note that generally bigger fundamental factors are necessary to break longer channels. It is likely that something far more significant is happening when a pair makes a new three-month high than if it makes a three-day high.

This is a critical concept. Generally, we can gauge the power of the move by the length of the breakout. It takes a bigger fundamental change in a market to make a new 52-week high than a new five-day high. I pay much more attention to new 52-week highs than five-day highs. Take note of this concept!

I'm going to show you how to trade channel breakouts, including my own enhancements.

WHAT IS A CHANNEL BREAKOUT?

A *channel breakout* is simply a breakout of the high or low of a certain number of days in the past. For example, to find the entry and exit points for a 20-day channel breakout, you look back over the last 20 days of price and identify the highest price and the lowest price during that period of time. Those are your initial buy or sell points. You put in a buy order just above the 20-day high and a sell order just under the 20-day low.

Let's assume you are not filled on the first day. On the next day, you go back 20 days and again identify the high and low for that period. Most days, the 20-day high and low will not change. You do this every day to define a new 20-day high price and a 20-day low price. Every day, you would put in a new buy order just above the new 20-day high and a sell order just below the new 20-day low.

Eventually, you will be filled on either the long or the short side. Your initial stop is the entry order on the other side of the channel. For example, you are trading EUR/USD and the 20-day high is 1.50 and the 20-day low is 1.40. I like to buy three pips above the breakout level. So in this case, you enter an order to buy at 1.5003 and an order to sell at 1.3997. The price trades up to 1.5003 and you are filled on the long side. Your original stop loss is 1.3997, which means that the original sell order now acts as your stop loss. You don't have to do anything. Just leave that original sell order with your broker.

Once you are filled on the long side, in this example, place a new order to sell at 1.3997. Now you will have two orders to sell at 1.3997. You need to do this because the first order there will exit the long position but you need the second order to get you short. Classic channel breakouts are always in the market, either long or short.

Let's look at Figure 3.1 to bring this to life. I've selected this chart because it shows both trending and nontrending markets. It shows both typical winning and losing trades.

The chart shows the British Pound from March through November. I've put a 20-day channel on the chart. Remember, the 20-day channel on any given day is simply the highest and lowest price for the previous 20 days. At the end of every day, you will put in orders to buy slightly above the 20-day high and sell slightly below the 20-day low.

Early in April, the Pound dropped below the 20-day low, thus triggering a sell signal getting us short on the Pound. We already have in an order to buy above the 20-day high but we add another similar order to make sure that we get long if the Pound rises above the 20-day high. Remember, we are always in the market using the classic channel breakout technique. So if the price traded up to above the 20-day high, we would get stopped out on our short position but also go long. That means that we need to have two buy orders above the 20-day high.

The market continued down over the next week and our trade looked good. Note that our stop at the 20-day high doesn't change for almost two weeks. That's because the highest price for each of those days didn't change. However, in mid-May, the top line representing the 20-day high finally started to drift lower. You would lower the protective stop and the long buy order each time that the 20-day high moves lower.

The Pound then drifted sideways through the end of April but broke down again in early May. The price of the Pound started to rally in mid-May. It rallied almost up to the top line of the channel but never surmounted it. The Pound then dipped down to the 20-day low in mid-June. That dip

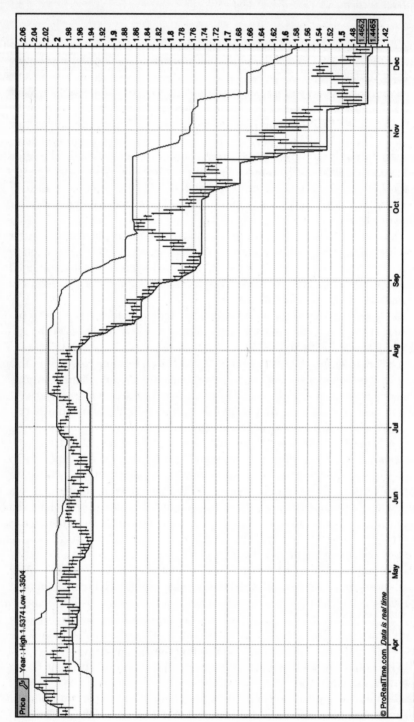

FIGURE 3.1 British Pound

was followed by a rally that eventually caused a break of the 20-day high line near the end of June. You would be stopped out of the previous short position and would also get long. You would have lost about 250 pips on the short position and be long with a stop at the 20-day low line.

We get a few days of follow-through but the market then turns lower into early July. The market then hits a new high in mid-July and we are thinking we are genius traders. We also are raising our stop just about every day during this time as the 20-day low line increases.

However, the market then starts to drop and we get stopped out and go short very early in August. This trade loses us about 200 pips.

The market then plunges at the beginning of September. The stop loss is starting to move lower but is still very high above the current price. We are up about 1,900 pips on a mark-to-market basis. But then a sharp rally starts in the early part of September that hits the top of the 20-day channel in the third week of September where we are stopped out with a profit of about 1,000 pips and go long at the same time.

That position would then be stopped out in the first week of October for a loss of about 1,200 pips and we would also go short at the same time. We would still be short with an open profit of about 2,200 pips at the end of the chart.

This technique would be called the 20/20 system because we use the 20-day high/low to enter the position and the 20-day high/low to exit the position. Note that the 20/20 is essentially Donchian's four-week rule (4WR), since there are 20 days in four weeks.

We would have ended up being profitable during this period of time but it would have been an aggravating profit. We'll make some enhancements to the system to improve it.

I don't recommend using this system. I just wanted to show the concept of channel breakouts using the simple four-week rule. The 20/20 system is profitable, but there are other superior methods you can use.

BETTER CHANNEL BREAKOUTS

Over time, investors discovered that the simple 4WR could be enhanced. A big change was to make it not always in the market; the system could be sometimes in the market, but there would be times that it would not be in the market. In other words, the 4WR was always in the market. You were either long or short all the time. So the first enhancement was to create a system similar to the 4WR but was not always long or short. It could instead be long, short, or flat.

The second enhancement was to change the length of the channels. It turns out that longer channels can work much better for timing entries.

In the late 1980s I started using what I called the 40/20. When there was a break of the 40-day high or low, we entered long and short positions. The 40/20 was the same system as the 4WR, except that the time was twice as long. You could say that entries were made using an eight-week rule. However, the exits were on a break of the 20-day high or low depending on whether you were long or short. This meant, for example, that you would enter long when the market made a new 40-day high and you would exit that trade when it made a new 20-day low. Note that you did not go short when the market made a new 20-day low; you only exited your existing long position. You would be flat the market if you got stopped out. This is different from the classic channel breakout. With the classic channel breakout, you are always in the market while the new method has you on the sidelines.

This was a major breakthrough in channel trading. Often a market would be in a nice strong rally and then quickly dip to the bottom and get short on what was really just a retracement in a major bull market. The rally on the British Pound chart (Figure 3.1) in September is an excellent example. In hindsight, we wouldn't want to get long on that break to new highs. We would have preferred to stand aside. I'll show you how to avoid those dings later.

I used the 40/20 for many years. Studies and my own experience showed it to be a nicely profitable system.

I later changed to a 55/20 after the release of the Turtle System to the public. The Turtles were a group of traders trained by legendary traders Richard Dennis and William Eckhardt. They were basically trend followers and their core techniques were channel breakouts. They had settled on 55/20 parameters. The Turtles were some of the most profitable traders, so I was intrigued to find out that they were users of channel breakouts. In addition to using 55/20, they were also using the classic 4WR!

I love to learn, particularly from great traders. Dennis and Eckhardt certainly fit that description, having made hundreds of millions of dollars by the mid-1980s. It was amazing that they achieved that much success using the old-fashioned 4WR.

But they had also found out that using a longer-term entry parameter combined with a shorter-term exit parameter was an improvement over the classic 4WR. They had also created other rules for trading but this was the core upon which everything else was measured.

I had not checked which parameters were best so I tested whether the 55-day parameter was better than my 40-day parameter. It was! Actually, just about everything between 50 to 60 days had about the same results. So I enhanced my trading by switching to the parameters that the Turtles were using. Basically, I was shifting from a two-month breakout to almost a three-month breakout. I was going to be trading less often but presumably entering only when there was a monster move in place.

To repeat: Entries are made using 55 days but exits are made with 20 days. Let's look at an example. Figure 3.2 is the same chart as shown in Figure 3.1, but now I've added a 55-day channel. If the 20 and the 55 channel high and/or low are the same, then you will only see one line. An example of this is the month of July. The top channel for both the 20-day and 55-day high are exactly the same so you only see one line. But note that there are two lines below the prices. The higher line is the 20-day low line and the bottom line is the 55.

Let's follow the same process we did earlier but this time add in the 55-day parameter.

First, note that we do not get short in early April but wait until early May. This shows a couple of things. First, 55-day breakouts will occur far less often than 20-day breakouts. In this case, the market had to drop for another month to create a strong enough bear market to trigger the 55-day low. Second, this actually hurt us in this trade because we sold at a price lower than we would have using the 20-day low. On the other hand, I actually don't mind the lower price for the entry because it means that I didn't have my money tied up for about a month with a market going nowhere. I don't want to invest in things that are going sideways. It's a waste of time and attention.

We get short then in early May and get stopped out when the market moves above the 20-day high near the end of June for a loss of about 450 pips. Ugh. Now we are on the sidelines, not long. The market then moves sideways and then breaks the 55-day high and gets us long in the middle of July. That trade quickly fails and we are stopped out right at the beginning of August for about a 650-pip loss. A few days later, we get short when we break the 55-day low on August 8. The market then collapses and we show a profit until the sharp rally stops us out near the end of September. We still make about a 750-pip profit. We get short again in early October and would be showing a nice profit as the chart ends.

Note that this shift to 55 days eliminated the short position in early June. We lost a little more on the losing trades than when we used the 4WR, but we were able to eliminate one of the losing trades. We are probably a little bit more profitable by adding in this new, longer entry channel. Over the long run, we will be much more profitable.

A lot of people ask me what will happen if these two parameters become very popular. Won't that degrade the performance?

There is no question that a method can become too popular and the performance begins to degrade. But this technique is robust. First, few traders are looking at 55-day highs. Most traders are using short-term support and resistance to time their trades. They are looking at 10-day moving

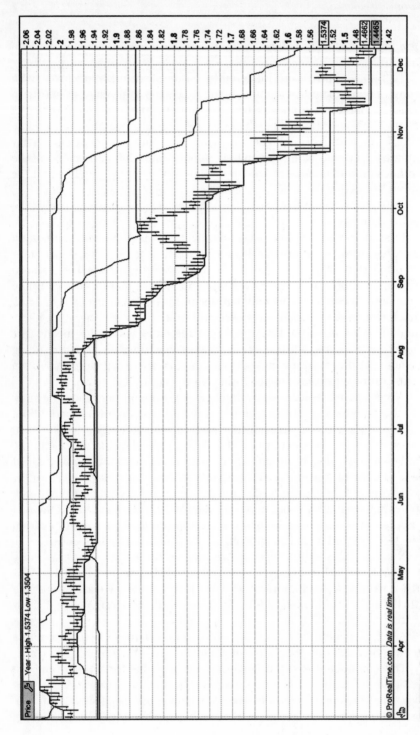

FIGURE 3.2 British Pound with Channels Added

averages and the most recent high or low. Few are looking back over the last 55 days. Still, it is possible that the 55-day high or low could have occurred in the last 10 days and that means that a lot of traders will be looking at that point to buy or sell, which will degrade performance slightly. I'm always concerned about dealers and other short-term traders moving a price to just above the 55-day high, triggering stops, and then having the market collapse. The breakout will have occurred due to short-term price manipulation rather that a significant change in the fundamentals. I'll tell you how we can counteract that next.

The 55/20 technique is so robust that you can use just about any parameter between 50 and 60. If you think that everyone is entering on 55-day highs and lows then shift to 54 or 56. Heck, you can go all the way to 50- or 60-day highs or lows and it won't make any difference. The basic technique is catching some deep human action; shifting the parameters slightly won't change the performance.

In addition, 55/20 are not necessarily the optimal parameters for each pair at all times. The best overall parameter is 55/20 because it works the best for all pairs over the longest period of time.

I've found that the use of 20 days for the exit works well for most pairs most of the time so I don't fiddle with it. However, I have seen the optimal length of the entry channel range from about 30 to about 70. I've seen the optimal entry parameter change from year to year by half or double.

The problem with constantly changing the entry parameter is that you will always be using the parameter that worked over the recent past, not the parameter that will work in the near future. Sure, a parameter that worked the best last month or year will likely be the parameter that will work the best in the coming month or year. But I don't like to fiddle with the parameters because it makes the method less accountable and effectively turns the trading method into a discretionary method. I'll talk more about this concept in Chapter 9 on the psychology of trading. Chasing varying parameters is generally a waste of time. Finding a strong and robust set of parameters that works is the key and I've presented those parameters.

THE PROS AND CONS OF CHANNEL BREAKOUTS

The biggest argument in favor of channel breakouts is that they are extremely profitable. They are the core technique used by the most profitable traders. That alone should be enough to convince you to use this technique. I recognize that my job is to make money, not to be brilliant or creative or even right. It's to make money. So I want to use techniques that make money and the channel breakout technique makes money.

One of the key advantages of channel breakouts is that you are guaranteed to catch the big moves in the pair. The big money is made on the big moves so a huge advantage of channel breakouts is that they participate in every big move. This advantage can't be underestimated. It is this attribute that drives great traders to use channel breakouts. You can't make serious money trading without making sure you are on board with the big moves.

Yes, the method can get chopped up with a sideways market but even here the method works well. Having to make a new 55-day high or low cuts down on the whipsaws. It usually takes a strong move in the market to make a new 55-day high or low. That provides some protection against any possible false breakout. But don't fear, I will discuss the ways to protect against serious losses using channel breakouts.

The main disadvantage with the channel breakout technique is that the stop loss is a long way from the entry point. I haven't talked about risk management yet (see Chapter 7), but let me just say that the wider the stop, the smaller your position will be if you have a position at all. In other words, you can't take a normal-size position because the risk is so high due to the distance of the entry price to the exit channel. Getting stopped out is a painful experience because of the distance between the entry and exit channels. So what we need to do is to enhance the rules of channel breakouts to improve performance and reduce risk.

THE BISHOP

My first enhancement is to use the Bishop to trigger liquidation signals. Take a look at Figure 3.3. I have taken Figure 3.2 and added the average directional index (ADX) indicator at the bottom. As you can see, the Bishop gave us two good signals. I've put the cursor on the first signal to make it easy to see.

Note that we exit right near the low of the major move down and move to the sidelines just before the rally that caused the standard rules for channel breakouts to be stopped out. The standard rules state that we exit only when we hit the 20-day high. Adding the Bishop actually allows us to exit, in this case, near the bottom of the major move down and before the significant rally in September. This timely exit adds about 1,000 pips to our profits for the year.

Remember that the Bishop is showing that the trend has ended. It triggers a buy signal in this case just a couple of days before the actual low in the move. This is a huge enhancement to the profits for the year.

The next signal is not as good. Figure 3.4 shows the next Bishop exit signal near the end of the chart. We have exited smartly, but we would have

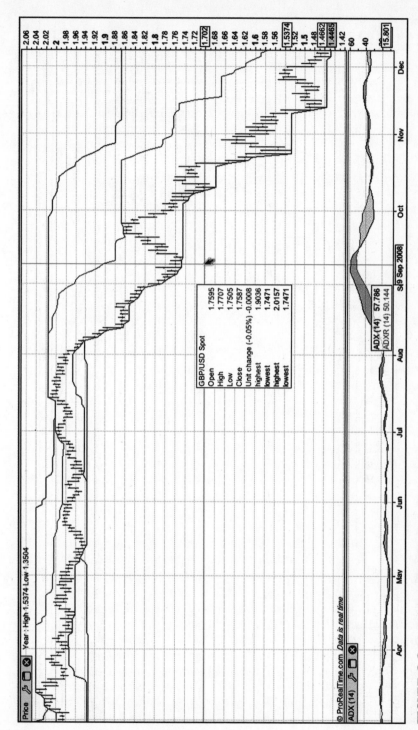

FIGURE 3.3 British Pound with ADX Added

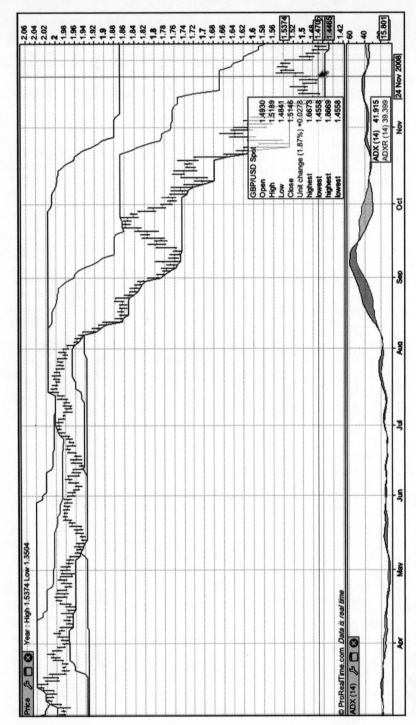

FIGURE 3.4 British Pound with Bishop Signal

been slightly better off if we had stayed in the trade. Not bad but not good either.

In any case, the net result of adding the Bishop exit signal is a major improvement to profitability for the year. I think this is a good example because it has one big winner and one small loser, which is typical of the Bishop. It will make some amazing calls that add to our bottom line but then will have a signal that hurts us slightly. The net result is still a big winner.

ADX FILTER

My next enhancement to the basic channel breakout is to add the ADX filter that I introduced in the previous chapter. Let's take a new look at the GBP/USD chart in Figure 3.5. This figure shows the ADX across the bottom of the chart. It turns out that every one of the trading signals occurred while the ADX was rising. As a result, the ADX filter never eliminated any trades.

In Figure 3.6, the chart has been moved to the right so that you can see the more recent price action. I've put the cursor on December 4 where the market breaks down. Also note the breakdown just at the end of December. The ADX was declining in both cases so we would not have taken either of these trades. As the chart shows, there was no real follow-through on either of these trades. The ADX filter saved us from the sharp rally to the 20-day high where we would have been stopped out for a loss of over 800 pips. The ADX filter helped us dodge a bullet.

The ADX filter would have gotten us out of the trade at the end of December as well. This would have saved us a little money because we would have stopped ourselves out due to a new technique I'm going to show you next. But I still wouldn't have minded not entering that trade anyway. The market moved sharply higher and I would have been suffering mightily for a couple of weeks until the market finally broke down in the middle of January. I would have preferred not to enter this trade and instead get in a little lower in the middle of January.

Using an ADX filter means that we will be trading slightly less often because, by definition, some of the trades will be not entered because at least some of the time the ADX will be moving lower. Our profits, however, are greatly enhanced because we will usually eliminate taking on some losing trades. Rarely will we be eliminating a profitable trade. It's no big deal if we eliminate a winning trade because we will get in at a slightly lower price. Remember, if the market breaks through the 55-day high/low and the ADX is declining, we will look to get in on the next breakout, which only requires one countertrend move. For example, we break to a new

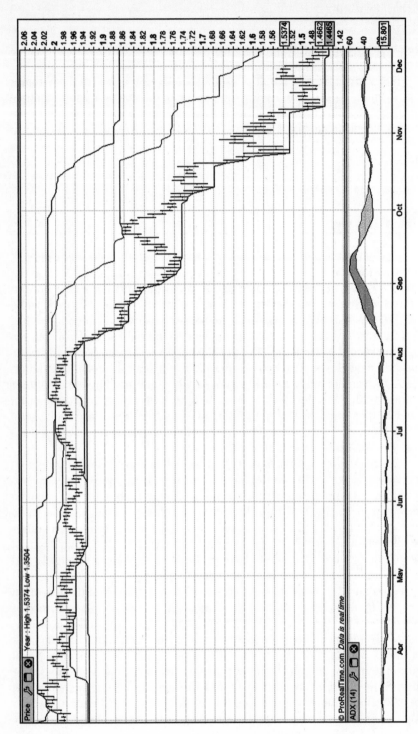

FIGURE 3.5 British Pound with ADX Filter

44

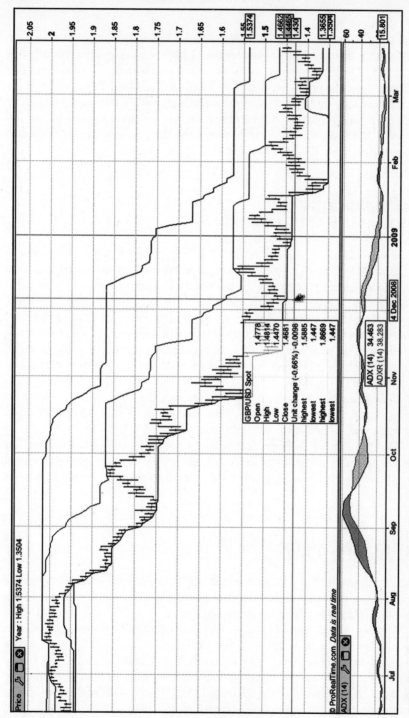

FIGURE 3.6 ADX Indicator Is Declining as Market Breaks Down

55-day high but the ADX is declining. We don't take the trade. But the market follows through and moves higher. I just need one day with a lower close to set up a new potential 55-day-high buy signal. We never want to put ourselves in a position where we don't catch the big move just because the ADX is moving lower. Any follow-through after a missed 55-day entry signal will likely lead the ADX to move higher so any subsequent buy signals will be triggered. We might have missed the first few days of the move but we won't miss the big part of the move.

THE PRINCIPLE OF INSTANT GRATIFICATION

I believe that one of the key underlying principles of profitable trading is the principle of instant gratification. This means that we should show a profit from the very beginning of the trade. Think back to your most profitable trades. Weren't they profitable from the very beginning of the trade or just after that? I think that my losing trades were nearly always losers from the first day on, too. Basically, you can almost predict whether or not a trade will be profitable by the price action of the first couple of days. We must always find ways to make sure that we are profitable from the beginning of the trade.

This principle is one of the reasons that I prefer to be a buyer on strength and seller on weakness. This sharply increases the chances that my trade will be profitable from the start.

The flip side of this principle is that I don't like to hold positions that are losing money. I want to get out before they become bigger losers. I don't want to wait around to see if they turn into winners. I want to get out right away.

REJECTION RULE

This leads me to the next enhancement to the classic channel breakout method: the rejection rule. This rule is designed to ensure that we are in sync with the principle of instant gratification.

Markets break out of support and resistance all the time. Sometimes the market will follow through and we will have a winning trade. Other times the market will fail and fall back below the breakout level. The question is whether the breakout was a false breakout or a premature breakout. A *false breakout* is a breakout that simply fails and never shows any follow-through. A *premature breakout* is a breakout that initially fails but eventually succeeds. The bulls needed to build more power before they could overwhelm the bears. Breakouts cannot be predicted but we want to protect ourselves against any sort of breakout that has no follow-through.

I call this rule the rejection rule because markets will reject a price if the price is too high or low for current conditions. The price may break out above a 55-day high but then move back to below the breakout level. In this case, the market has rejected the new high. The bears are able to quickly mount a counterattack and reject the breakout. The bulls do not have enough strength to keep the market above the breakout level.

Take a look at Figure 3.7, which focuses on just one short period of the previous figures. An arrow indicates the breakout that we want to view.

The first part of the rejection rule is the five-day condition. I want to see that the 55-day high has been flat or declining for at least five days prior to the breakout (use the opposite for breakdowns). The five-day condition ensures that we don't apply the rejection rule to markets that are running strongly up or down. We only want to use the rejection rule when the market is roughly sideways. We want to find all the reasons in the world to hang onto a position when the market is running. We want to look for reasons to bail out if the market is going sideways. So we only apply the rejection rule when the five-day condition is in place.

Figure 3.7 shows that the five-day condition is in place. The 55-day channel has been flat for over five days when the breakout comes on July 15 (see arrow). The rejection rule is now in place.

The rejection rule is simple: If a five-day condition is in place, liquidate a 55-day buy signal if the price of the market closes below the initial breakout level on the day of the breakout or the next day. In other words, the price must close above the breakout level for the first two days of the trade or you will exit on the close. If you can't exit on the close for whatever reason—for example, if you have a job that doesn't allow you to watch the markets during the day—then exit as soon as possible.

Let's take another look at Figure 3.7. The market has broken above the 55-day high on the day highlighted with the arrow. In this case, the market opened below the 55-day high but broke through during the day. First, we want to check to see if the market closes above the breakout level of the 55-day high on this first day. In this case, the market closes above the 55-day high so there is no rejection. However, the price closes below the breakout level on the second day of the trade so we exit the trade immediately.

- We are still looking at the original 55-day breakout level that caused us to initiate the trade, not the new 55-day high created by the breakout day.

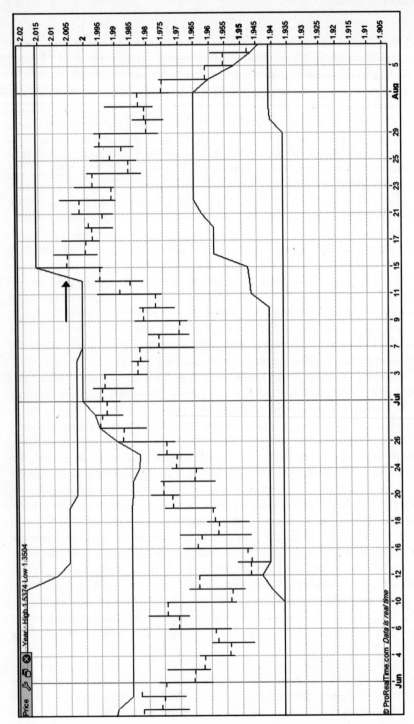

FIGURE 3.7 British Pound with Rejection Rule Highlighted (Arrow)

48

- Our loss in this trade is miniscule. We entered at a level just above 2.0000 and exited just slightly below that level. The loss is so small that it is hardly worth considering.
- But note that we would have been stopped out at about 1.9650 for a loss of about 350 pips if we were not using the rejection rule. The rejection rule saved us a lot of money, which is what it is designed to do.

This trade aligns with the principle of instant gratification. The trade failed right away. It made a profit for one day but it sold off a lot from the high of the day of the breakout. It only made money for one day, then failed. I have found throughout the years that it is better to eliminate trades that fail quickly rather than hope that they will eventually come back into profit.

The rejection rule significantly improves the profitability of the classic channel breakout method because it eliminates a lot of trades that would otherwise be stopped out at the 20-day low for a much larger loss. My experience is that roughly half of the normal stop-outs are eliminated by the use of the rejection rule. This is a significant enhancement over the classic channel breakout.

I'll talk about risk management in Chapter 7, but let me just point out that the risk per contract is greatly reduced by the rejection rule. Now, the risk on a trade will rarely be the 20-day low. Instead, it will be a risk that is unknown but likely close to the entry price. Note that it was only a few pips away from the entry price in the example in this chapter. The risk will usually be greater than our example, which is a common example.

Think for a minute. You might normally allocate a certain amount of risk to each trade. Let's say you want to risk $1,000 on each trade. Let's further say that it will be a $1,000 loss if the 20-day low is hit. The rejection rule will kick in before the 20-day low in most cases. That is the result of the principle of instant gratification. Let's assume that you lose $200 every time you get stopped out on the rejection rule rather than the $1,000 that you lose if you hit the 20-day low. This means that you can either cut your risk by 80 percent or increase your profit fivefold. (Remember that this is just an estimate.) This is a dramatic change to the risks and rewards that come from the channel breakout method. Let's explore this further.

Let's assume that you want to cut risk by 80 percent. You will have a higher number of losing positions compared with the classic channel breakout. The rejection rule creates a stop that is close to the entry position. The closer a stop is to the current market, the more often it will be hit. It is not often that you will hit a stop that is the 20-day low. So you should expect to get stopped out fairly frequently. However, the average size of your losing trades will shrink dramatically. In our example, we will be stopped out more often but our stop will limit our loss to only one-fifth of the loss of getting stopped out at the 20-day low. The net result of a higher number of losing trades with a sharply lower size of losing trades equals a big boost to our bottom line.

Alternately, you could put on a position five times larger than you would normally. Okay, perhaps not that aggressive. But you could easily double or triple the size of your position and still take on less risk than you would using the normal channel breakout method. You would take the normal $1,000 risk on your position but receive double or triple the profits on winning trades!

Let's look back at Figure 3.7. Find the day before the actual breakout. The market was very close to the 55-day high so we could put in an order to buy at 3 pips higher than the 55-day high. Where will the initial stop be? We know that we are going to put in a stop at the 20-day low but we also know that we will be getting out at a much higher price should the rejection rule kick in. In this case, we need to determine where we would be stopped out should the rejection rule kick in. Of course, we never know where it will kick in but we need to estimate this so that we can figure out the size of our upcoming positions.

Let's say that we figure that we will be stopped out no lower than 1.9850 should the rejection rule be triggered. That is about one-third the dollar risk of actually trading down to the 20-day low. So, we can say that the dollar risk using the rejection rule is one-third of the risk of using the 20-day low. However, we will be stopped out on a slightly larger number of trades so we need to scale the dollar risk higher to take into account the additional number of stop-outs. So, let's estimate that we will lose 50 percent less using the rejection rule than using the 20-day low. We must now decide whether we want to reduce our risk by 50 percent and only trade one contract or trade two contracts, which would boost the risk to 100 percent of the 20-day low but would double our profits should the trade work. In order to make this decision, the background environment must be taken into consideration. For example, is this trade in the direction of the long-term trend? What are the expected seasonal price tendencies? Do you have a fundamental bias? Are there any conflicting or supporting technical indicators?

If the bias from these other factors is bearish, then you should probably just put on the one contract and cut your risk while maintaining the normal profits potential. If the bias is bullish from these other environmental factors, then you should probably double the size of the position, take the normal level of risk, but have double the profit potential.

Once again, you now have the flexibility of either cutting risk and leaving the profit potential the same or keeping the risk the same and making more money. This is a major enhancement to the classic channel breakout.

Adding the rejection rule adds significantly to the classic channel breakout. But there are two drawbacks. The first is that we don't really know where the risk is. We don't really know at what price the rejection rule will be triggered. This makes risk management a problem. Second, the rejection rule only covers the first two days we are in a trade. Do we really want to let our stop drop down to the 20-day low after the first two days in the trade? What if we were aggressive and bought a double-size position? Now the risk has ramped up dramatically and we may have a much larger position than we would want with a stop loss at the 20-day low.

THE LAST BAR TECHNIQUE

The solution to this risk management problem is the last bar technique.

I originally got this idea from ace trader Peter Brandt. I had the opportunity to interview him and read his book *Trading Futures with Classical Chart Patterns* (Advanced Trading Seminars, 2000). He used classical chart formations such as head and shoulders and trendlines. He used the chart patterns as outlined in Magee and Edwards' excellent book *Technical Analysis of Stock Trends* (AMACOM, 1997). There is actually a chapter on trading futures in that book. The problem with Magee and Edwards is that they suggested that you enter, for example, a head and shoulders top on a break of the neckline with a stop above the right shoulder. This would be a very wide stop and Brandt felt that proper risk management would mean that he would never be able to enter any trades.

So what Brandt did was to put his stop, to carry on this example, above the high of the last bar in the formation. His concept was that the market had broken below support. It should be unlikely that the market would trade back up through the neckline and even go further and break the high of the last day in the formation. That would be two levels of resistance that should cap any rallies, particularly if the trade was going to be a winner. Brandt is using the principle of instant gratification here.

Following Brandt's idea, I apply it to the channel breakout technique. Let's keep looking at our British Pound example in Figure 3.7. In this case, the market broke the 55-day high on July 15. Note that the bar of the 15th is the last bar with any portion still under the 55-day level. We set our stop loss at the bottom of this bar.

Let's assume for a moment that we are not using the rejection rule. That means that our initial stop loss in this trade would be the low of the bar of July 15, or about 1.9940. We would have been stopped out three days later at that level for a loss of about 80 pips. No big deal.

I will use the second-to-last bar if the last is barely below the break-out level or it gaps above the breakout level. We are trying to find the last bar or near-last bar that defines where support will come in if the market sets back into the range. There is a certain level of discretion necessary to determine the best "last bar." Most of the time, we can simply use the true last bar as our stop. We look for the bar that was the breakout bar. That should be the last bar 98 percent of the time. Only rarely are we going to look back one more bar to be the last bar.

TACTICS

There are four different exit strategies for the channel breakout method. Let's assume that we have bought the British Pound. We will look at the rejection rule as our stop on the first two days we are in the trade. We will then shift to the last-bar method after the first two days. We will look at the Bishop starting from the first day and will keep it in mind every day we have the trade open. Finally, we will use the 20-day low once the 20-day low is higher than the low of the last bar. To repeat: First look at the rejection rule, then the last bar, then the 20-day low, in that order. We are looking at the Bishop every day.

You should be putting in both buy and sell orders every day if you have no position. Once you are in a position, you need to put in your protective stops depending on the method you are following.

TAKING PROFITS

One of the key advantages of these enhancements is that it allows you to sometimes exit positions near the high of moves. I showed you how the Bishop enabled us to exit with a huge profit in September. Let's look at some other trades.

Refer back to Figure 3.3. I had previously marked the Bishop exit. That was a great exit and created a huge profit. We get short at the beginning of October. Notice that the rejection rule kicks in on the second day in the trade and we take a microscopic loss. But we enter short on the third day as we break down again. This trade has no five-day condition so there is no opportunity for the rejection rule to come into play. So we get short and use the last-bar technique as our initial stop loss. We never get stopped out so we shift from using the last bar to the 20-day high near the beginning of November when the 20-day high finally moves to below the level of the last bar. But before that, we get another breakdown in the middle of October.

There is a five-day condition in place so there is a potential rejection rule. However, prices slam lower and the rejection rule is never triggered. But it does cause a new lower last bar, which could become our new stop loss but I prefer to use the 20-day high.

I prefer to use the 20-day high after I have a nice profit because it is best to give a profitable trade lots of room to make more money. You may want to move the stop on part of the position to the new last bar. Still, this should be a small percent of the total position. Use the 20-day high to make sure that you are maximizing the big money. So we remain short.

But take a look in the lower-right corner of the chart. Note that there is a five-day condition in place on that breakdown two bars from the end of the chart. Notice that rejection rule kicks in and we exit the trade. At this point, we got short in early October near 1.7400 and exit near 1.4750 for a monster profit. More important, the rejection rule gets us out of the position on the absolute low bar on the chart. What perfect timing! There are few techniques that can get us out of positions so close to the absolute low of the move. So the rejection rule, and the last bar, will help to get us out of trades and take profits near the lowest or highest price in the move. This is a huge enhancement of the classic channel breakout.

Basically, we have taken probably the most powerful profit-generating system in trading and added some strong enhancements that reduce the risk, enhance profitability, and allow us to often take profits near highs rather than waiting for the trend to reverse.

THE BOTTOM LINE

If you only use one technique from this book, use the channel breakout method. But make sure that you use my enhancements, too! I believe that more money has been made using this technique in futures and forex than any other technique. The technique can be used plain vanilla or easily enhanced using the methods discussed in this chapter.

CHAPTER 4

The Conqueror

T his chapter discusses the Conqueror, which is a clever method that encourages some truly original thinking. I am a big fan of trading through multiple time frames (see Chapter 10 for more information on diversifying through time). This particular method looks at three different time frames before entering a trade.

Most methods use the same method for entering and exiting trades. For example, you buy when the 20-day moving average crosses above the 50-day moving average and sell when the 20-day moving average crosses below the 50-day moving average. However, the Conqueror actually uses a different exit technique from the entry technique. This is rare in the world of trading.

In previous chapters we've covered ways to exit a trade that are different from the entry point. This uncommon approach leads to much higher profits than the basic method that most people use to trade. The Conqueror uses one method to enter and another method to exit. They are related to each other but are separate. In addition, the stop loss is adaptive. That is, it looks at current market conditions and adapts to those conditions to create the exit strategy.

THE BEGINNINGS OF THE CONQUEROR

The idea originated back in 1991 when Bruce Babcock created a system called the Currency Conquistador. Bruce was one of the pioneers of futures trading. He was the founder of *Commodity Traders Consumer Report*

(CTCR, which is now Web-only at www.ctcr.investors.net), which I bought from him in 1996 when he was diagnosed with cancer. He was the author of one of the most popular books on trading, *Dow Jones-Irwin Guide to Trading Systems*, and designed many profitable systems.

Perhaps his greatest contribution to futures trading was a sense of integrity and cutting through the hype that fills the futures and forex world. CTCR allowed no advertising so Bruce could be totally honest in his reviews of products.

Bruce fiddled with the Currency Conquistador for a few years and then released Currency Conquistador II. This presented a more sensitive stop loss method than the first version.

At this point, ace researcher Nelson Freeburg enters the story. Nelson publishes an amazing newsletter called *Formula Research* (see Appendix: Suggested Reading for more information). Nelson develops trading methods and systems for trading most markets. He has a clever mind and has come up with some great systems. I highly recommend his publication.

Nelson published an enhancement for the Conquistador at the end of 1994. One key enhancement was that the original Currency Conquistador was only for trading currencies. Nelson broadened the testing to other futures contracts and found that his modifications made it profitable for a broad list of futures. We are only looking at forex in this book, but knowing that the method works on many more markets gives confidence that this is a strong method.

Nelson also simplified the system, which is almost always a good thing. In this case, it was a good thing because Nelson-simplified systems outperformed the basic Babcock system.

WHAT IS TRUE RANGE?

Before I get into the mechanics of the system, let me first discuss *true range* as we will be using this concept in the calculation of the Conqueror.

One of the advantages of the forex market is that the opening price is basically the same as the closing price of the previous day. We close at one price and the opening price is simply the next tick. The only exception is the close on Friday going over to the open on Monday. Here, it is possible for a gap to be created by the change in price occurring over the weekend. In this case, we need to adjust for the potential gap in figuring out the true range on Monday. We will know what the actual range is by simply looking at the chart or a table and seeing what your chart service tells you what the range is. Good enough. The problem comes in when there is a gap between the range on Friday and the range on Monday.

In this case, the reported range doesn't really represent the range of the day. Let's say that the price gapped down and the high on Monday is below the low of Friday. The range that is reported is not reflective of what implicitly happened. Although no trading occurred between the high of Monday and the close of Friday, it can be said that the true high for Monday should have been the close of Friday.

Here is how Nelson defined it in CTCR in 1995:

To begin with, a day's true high is the higher of today's high or yesterday's close. The true low is the lower of today's low or yesterday's close.

The true range is simply the true high minus the true low. The true range is designed to better measure the totality of price movement in cases where yesterday's close lies beyond today's price range.

Table 4.1, reproduced from *Commodity Traders Consumer Report*, shows the results of Nelson's final modification of the Conquistador.

As you can see, the method is very profitable. In fact, here is what Nelson stated in his issue of *Formula Research* devoted to the Conquistador:

The self-adjusting stop is perhaps the most innovative element in this versatile trading system. The wealth of applications inherent in the logic is a tribute to the analyst who designed it. We are in Bruce Babcock's debt for sharing Currency Conquistador, which, in terms of sheer dollars gained, is the most profitable futures system Formula Research *has published thus far.* (Commodity Traders Consumer Report, *1991*)

ENHANCING THE CONQUISTADOR

Now I enter the story. I took Nelson's profitable modifications of the Conquistador and modified them. I've created two different versions. One is *very* long term and the other is short term. To differentiate the results from the excellent work of Bruce and Nelson, I changed the name to the Conqueror.

Let's now take a look at the rules. First, we define several conditions. A positive number is bullish and a negative number is bearish.

1. Today's close minus the 10-day moving average (MA) of the close
2. Today's 10-day MA minus the 10-day MA 10 days ago
3. Today's close minus the close 40 days ago

TABLE 4.1 Currency Conquistador Version by Nelson Freeburg (Study Shows Profits/Losses from August 1, 1972, to July 9, 1998)

	Swiss Franc	British Pound	D-mark	Japanese Yen	Average
Total Net Profit	$167,062	$177,688	$112,675	$212,437	$167,466
Total Number of Trades	97	124	104	102	107
Number Winning Trades	45	46	52	53	49
Number Losing Trades	52	78	52	49	58
Percent Profitable	46 percent	37 percent	50 percent	51 percent	46 percent
Largest Winning Trade	$19,450	$32,018	$20,187	$32,662	$26,079
Largest Losing Trade	$(2,787)	$(3,019)	$(3,987)	$(3,087)	$(3,220)
Average Winning Trade	$5,669	$7,140	$3,633	$5,327	$5,442
Average Losing Trade	$(1,693)	$(1,933)	$(1,467)	$(1,426)	$(1,630)
Ratio Average Win/Average Loss	3.34	3.69	2.47	3.73	3.31
Average Trade (Win & Loss)	$1,722	$1,433	$1,083	$2,082	$1,580
Maximum Consecutive Winners	5	4	7	4	5
Maximum Consecutive Losers	5	9	4	3	5
Average Number of Bars in Winners	110	104	94	99	102
Average Number of Bars in Losers	23	15	25	21	21
Max Closed-Out Drawdown	$(8,000)	$(26,468)	$(7,475)	$(8,162)	$(12,526)
Max Intra-Day Drawdown	$(8,162)	$(26,725)	$(8,175)	$(9,237)	$(13,075)
Profit Factor	2.89	2.17	2.47	4.03	2.89
Account Size Required	$11,162	$29,725	$11,175	$12,237	$16,075
Return on Account	1,496 percent	597 percent	1,008 percent	1,735 percent	1,209 percent

Source: Commodity Traders Consumer Report, 1991.

Go long if all three conditions are positive. Go short if all three conditions are negative. Stand aside on any other condition. I'll get to the protective stop in a minute.

Let's consider this entry situation. Basically, we are looking at three different time horizons. First, we are looking at the price action over the last 10 days when we look at condition one. Condition two is really looking at the price action of the last 20 days. Finally, condition three is looking at the last 40 days.

We do not go long or short until all three trends in the market are congruent. The concept of applying three different time frames is unusual in trading. I had kind of a "doh" moment when I first saw it because it is so obvious yet never really done.

Basically, we are making sure that whatever trend is in place is powerful enough to turn all three directions bullish or bearish. A sideways market will not trigger the three conditions and we will stand aside in those situations, which is perfect. Only when the market really starts to move in one direction or another will the three trends line up and we will enter the market. Otherwise, one or more of the three conditions will be positive or negative and we will look for opportunities in other markets.

It is, therefore, difficult to get a buy or sell signal from the Conqueror. Most of the time it sits out of the market. It stubbornly waits for the market to really get going in one direction or another before it jumps in with a long or short position. This is one of the most important features of the Conqueror. It sits out when the market is drifting sideways or has only a slight trend. This saves a lot of money in whipsaw losses. It is also a significant improvement over most trading methods!

Let's take a look at an example. Let's pick up the action in the middle of September. The three conditions are mixed at that point. Let's follow the flow of the trade to see how it develops.

I've marked three arrows in Figure 4.1. The first arrow shows that condition three is negative. The close that day is below the close of the market 40 days previously.

Three days later, the price closes below the 10-day moving average, turning this condition negative. That's two conditions that are negative. We still can't go short because we need to have all three conditions negative before we can go short.

Take a look at the chart. At this point, the market has had a down move from the upper left of the chart. There was a rally in mid-September. At this point, we don't know if this is the beginning of a new bull market or simply a countertrend rally in the down trend. The market should probably be considered as roughly neutral. At this point, we have two conditions negative and one positive.

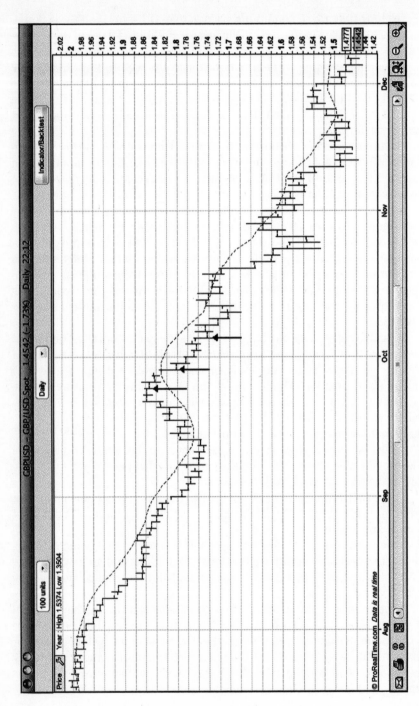

FIGURE 4.1 British Pound with Conditions Marked

The Conqueror sits back and waits until the trend is conclusively in one direction before entering. At this point, there are two negatives and one positive for only a net negative of one. This is not conclusive enough for the Conqueror.

The one condition that is not cooperating is the 10-day MA because it is still not below itself 10 days previously. It is not until early October before the 10-day MA drops enough. At that point, as the third arrow indicates, the third condition turns negative.

We go short on the close of trading on the day that the third condition triggers. If we don't know if the third condition has triggered until after the close of trading, then we go short on the open the following day. Okay, we are now short. All three conditions have been triggered. Where is our protective stop? Now it gets really interesting. We are going to use several different methods to determine the protective stop.

The first stop is a simple money management stop. For a standard contract, place a stop that would be a $2,000 loss. In other words, figure out how many pips represents $2,000 and place a stop that many pips away from the entry price. Fortunately, this stop will rarely be triggered. The other forms of stop will be triggered far more often. Still, we want some disaster insurance in place.

I've added another panel to the chart (see Figure 4.2). The new lower panel shows the average true range (ATR) over the past 40 days. This is simply the 40-day average of the ATR. You can see that the ATR was about 0.024 on the day we went short. That is really 240 pips. You can also see that the market was becoming more volatile from August through November. The ATR was slowly moving higher during this period showing that the average range for the day was increasing. In fact, it increased from about 150 pips per day to 350 pips per day.

This is the point where we create the two different versions of the Conqueror. Conqueror I will create a stop two times the ATR away from the current close while Conqueror II will create a stop 12 times the ATR away from the current close. Let's look closer at the current situation as an example.

Let's say that we get short at 1.7400. The ATR on that day is 0.0240, or 240 pips. Conqueror I will place a protective stop loss 480 pips above the lowest close in the move. On day one, the lowest close will be the close of the entry day. Every time the market makes a new lower close, you would change the stop.

In addition, you would also change the stop as the ATR changes. We started with an ATR of 240 pips but it eventually gets up to about 350 pips in November. That means that we would start by adding 480 pips to the lowest close but could be about 700 pips wide in November!

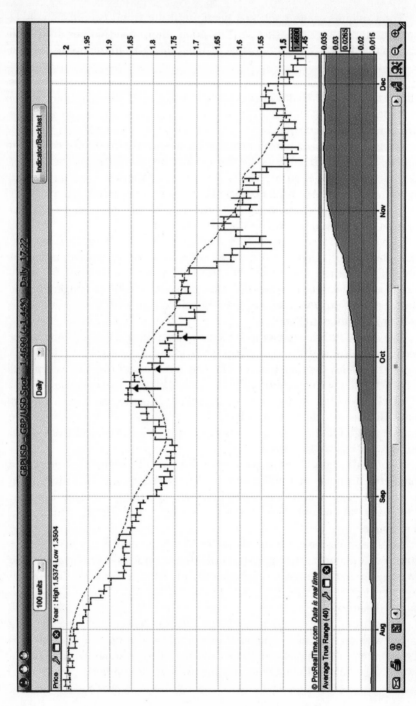

FIGURE 4.2 British Pound with ATR Added

I like this because it widens out the stop when the market is more volatile. That is perfect.

The day after the entry bar, which is marked with the third arrow, closes slightly up. We would keep the ATR stop at the same level. However, the next day shows a drop and a lower close. We would lower the stop to 480 above the new lower close. And so on.

Conqueror II uses the same idea except the stop is 12 times the ATR, or about 2,880 pips above the lowest close. That is a significant distance from the market so few traders will be able to trade it. I mention it here because it is a profitable method but challenging for anyone but the most highly capitalized to trade. I won't mention it again in this chapter. From now on, I'll only speak of the Conqueror as being Conqueror I.

ADJUSTING THE STOP

So far we have discussed two different stop loss techniques: the initial $2,000 money management stop and the two times ATR stop. Now comes the really interesting part.

We are going to adjust the ATR stop by how many conditions are in play. Remember that we went short when all three conditions were negative. Every time a factor changes sign (positive or negative), we will reduce the size of the ATR stop by a third. Let's work through an example.

We originally put on the trade in Figure 4.2 with a 480-pip stop. (I'm going to ignore subsequent changes in the ATR in our calculations but you shouldn't in the real world.) Note that all three conditions remain negative until the downward-pointing arrow in Figure 4.3. At that point, the price closes just barely above the 10-day MA, which turns that condition positive.

We take our 480-pip stop and deduct one-third of 480. One-third of 480 is 158 pips. We subtract 158 from 480, giving us a new trailing stop of 322. The lowest close occurs a couple of days before that at 1.7029. We place our new protective stop loss 322 pips above that at 1.7351. The price on that day does not stop us out but there is a spike higher two days after the down arrow and we are stopped out for a 24-pip loss.

We would not have been stopped out if we had continued with the original stop loss. It was wide enough to protect us from getting stopped out. Here, we got stopped out with a microscopic loss.

But the market turns down the next day and the market closes below the 10-day MA so all three conditions are negative again. We get short again on the close of that day at 1.7282. The ATR is exactly 250 on that day so our first stop is 500 pips above the close at 1.7282. So we now have a stop

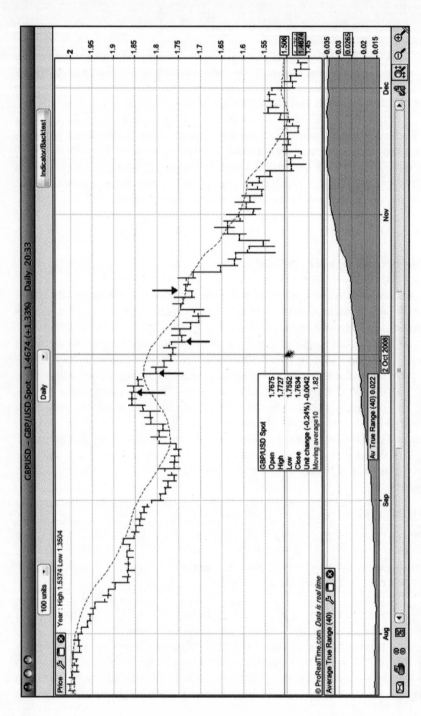

FIGURE 4.3 British Pound with Stop Adjustment Added

500 pips above the lowest close going forward until one or more of the conditions turn positive.

The market trades down to a low close four-fifths of the way through October at 1.5537. On that day, we lower the protective stop to 1.603 < 7, or 500 pips above the lowest close. We get stopped out the next day when the market moves up above 1.6057. We take a profit of over 1,200 pips.

At this point, all three conditions are still negative. That means that we could actually go short right away. However, I prefer to get a confirmation signal before reentering the short position. The best is that one of the conditions turns positive, then negative before we reenter the market. That occurs two days later when the market closes just above the 10-day MA, turning that condition positive. The market closes back below the 10-day MA the next day, turning this condition back to negative and all three conditions negative. Time to short the market again.

I won't carry the example along any further but you can see that the next trade was also profitable. One of the keys is that the Conqueror doesn't get involved in sideways markets. It sits patiently on the sidelines before getting involved. Also note that it moves the stop aggressively toward the current market price. Any significant retracement will stop out the Conqueror. It's a nervous system in that it leaps out of positions quickly when they go against the trade. It's hard to get into a Conqueror position but easy to get out.

It is also clear that the Conqueror loves a strong trend. It may get out quickly on a retracement but gets right back in if the three conditions reassert themselves. And they won't reassert themselves unless the three time frames are pointing in the same direction.

THE BOTTOM LINE

The Conqueror is a great technique that is being released to the general public in this book. This technique is based on systems designed by two of finest minds in this field, Bruce Babcock and Nelson Freeberg. That pedigree alone should make you want to try this method out.

This one-of-a-kind technique requires that a number of factors come to fruition before a long or short position is entered. At the same time, the Conqueror exits if the market hesitates just slightly. This means that the reward-to-risk ratio is superb.

CHAPTER 5

Stochastics

S tochastics are one of the most popular indicators. They are found on all the available chart services and software packages. They are a standard indicator in forex trading. But nearly everyone uses them incorrectly. I'll be focusing on bullish trades but everything also applies to the bearish trades.

WHAT ARE STOCHASTICS?

Stochastics are a form of oscillator. An oscillator measures the rate of change of prices. The simplest oscillator takes the current price and subtracts the price some number of days ago. For example, suppose EUR/USD closed today at 1.2050 and closed 10 days ago at 1.2000. The oscillator value would be 0.0050. This process would be repeated each day and plotted on a graph. The common wisdom is that oscillators will signal the turn in a market ahead of the actual turn in price because changes in momentum lead changes in the actual price. This idea follows the analogy of physics. The rate of change of an object will show decreasing momentum until the object actually changes direction.

The big criticism of oscillators is that they sometimes give a trading signal but the market is in such a strong trending mode that the signal is false. The common wisdom is that oscillators do well in nontrending markets and poorly in trending markets.

The simpler the oscillator, the more sensitive it is to current market price action. For example, a simple oscillator based on the 10-day rate of change will be more sensitive to current price action than an oscillator based on the 30-day rate of change.

Many analysts got beat up badly using the simple oscillators so they tried to find ways to improve them. Welles Wilder's relative strength index (RSI) and stochastics are the two most popular and famous improvements on the basic oscillator. Larry Williams's %R is actually the same as stochastics except not smoothed and the scale is turned upside down.

Stochastics are reasonably easy to calculate. There is a three-step process to calculate the two components of stochastics: %K and %D.

First calculate the raw stochastic number:

$$K = (C - L)/(H - L) * 100$$

Where C is the close of the last x number of days, H is the high for the last x number of days, and L is the low for the last x number of days. Typically, x is the last 14 days, though 9 days is also very popular.

%K is a three-day MA of K, and %D is a three-day MA of %K

Fortunately, you won't need to know the math unless you want to fiddle with it to see if you can improve it. Virtually all chart services, quote systems, and software packages have stochastics built in. However, they sometimes fiddle with the parameters. I suggest using the parameters I just outlined. The software packages and quote systems often allow you to change the parameters.

The one important question that must be addressed is the term of the stochastics. How many days will you use in your calculation? The classic answer is 14 days, which many people claim is about half of the normal cycle of forex prices. Other people use nine days, though I have never heard a justification for this number except that it is more sensitive than the usual 14 days. I have never seen any proof of the claim that the average price cycle is 28 days. Further, I have never seen any argument that you should, therefore, use a half cycle as your length in using stochastics. Nonetheless, fewer days in your calculations will lead to a more sensitive stochastic.

Could the length of stochastics be optimized? (By this I mean testing different parameters to find the most profitable one over a given test over past data.) Yes, but first you have to determine how you are going to use them. Are you going to use them as an overbought/oversold indicator? Are you going to use them as a trend indicator? Each use of stochastics will likely lead to a different optimization.

I won't get into the pros and cons of optimization here, so I suggest you read Bob Pardo's book on trading systems. See the Appendix for more information.

Unless otherwise stated, I will use 14 days as the length of the stochastics. Why? Well, I came up with all these profitable techniques when everything had to be done by hand and 14-day stochastics were all we had to use when testing. In the meantime, I have seen that these techniques work so I am loath to change them. I leave it to my superintelligent readers to optimize them!

A second reason to use 14 days for the length is that readers can easily use the indicators because they are the most common in available software packages. There is no need to fiddle with your software package to figure out how to change the parameters.

The techniques outlined in this chapter work similarly on both 9- and 14-day time frames. This is an important suggestion that stochastics are a robust indicator. However, the main difference between the 9- and 14-day stochastics is that the 9-day is more sensitive and gives more indications or signals. A key consideration in determining which length to use is your particular trading style. A longer length will give fewer signals and later signals but will filter out some whipsaws. A shorter length will give more signals and earlier signals but will be whipsawed more often.

Stochastics are essentially a measure of the close as related to the high and low. The stochastic measures the percent distance of the close to the range. Thus, a reading of 50 percent means that the close is halfway between the high and low. A reading of 75 percent means that the close was at the 75 percent level between the high and low. In other words, it was at the 75 percent level of the day's range or nearer to the high than the low. This means that you can only see a stochastic reading of 100 percent if a market closes on its high every day in the study. The underlying concept is that it is bullish if the market is tending to close in the upper half of the day's range and bearish if the converse is true.

Stochastics are used to trade all time frames, including day trading. Obviously, the most popular time frame is daily, using daily bars. However, I know a number of people who use them on shorter-term bars, such as five-minute and 60-minute bars. George Lane, the inventor of stochastics, used to use stochastics on three-minute bars in the S&P 500 futures.

HOW TO USE STOCHASTICS AS AN OVERBOUGHT AND OVERSOLD INDICATOR

Stochastics can be used as an overbought and oversold indicator. This is the most common use. The underlying idea is that a market will not normally move in one direction or the other for very long without running out of buyers, in a bull move, or sellers, in a bear move. If the market shoots up sharply, without a retracement, then the market is considered overbought. Conversely, a sharp drop in price, without a retracement, will lead to an oversold market.

The basic theory is that prices cannot go too far too fast. If they do, then they are ripe for a retracement. The retracement is necessary to "correct the overbought situation." A market that has shot up quickly has moved the price of the pair away from the underlying value too quickly. As a result, the market will set back slightly to induce more buying into the market.

The concept of overbought and oversold is mainly used to try to predict short-term price movements against the trend. It is also used to help dissuade traders from buying the market after the market has moved strongly. It is used to encourage traders to wait for a setback before buying.

In general, the concept of overbought and oversold works. Typically, when the stochastics get above 80 percent, the market is overbought; when stochastics get below 20 percent, the market is oversold. You should normally expect a correction to ensue relatively soon. This is the way that most people use stochastics. However, just because it generally works and calls corrections accurately doesn't mean that it is profitable. In fact, selling when stochastics get above 80 percent and buying when stochastics get below 20 percent is a money-losing strategy.

Some people modify the method and sell when the stochastics get above 80 percent and the %K crosses down below the %D and buy when the stochastics get below 20 percent and the %K crosses above the %D. This works better but is still a money-losing strategy.

The problem is strongly trending markets. Using stochastics as an overbought/oversold indicator falls completely apart. In other words, the concepts of overbought and oversold work during mild trends and sideways markets but do terribly during trending markets. In fact, some people have suggested that you are better off buying when the %K crosses above the 80 percent line and selling when the %K crosses down below the 20 percent line. This is actually better than what we have been talking about, but it also loses money.

First, you must determine what kind of trader you are before using stochastics as an overbought or oversold indicator. You should consider using stochastics if you are the type of trader who wants to buy dips and sell rallies in trendless markets, and is willing to lose when the market finally starts to trend. If you are a trend follower, then you should ignore the stochastic overbought and oversold reading. Stochastics will register an overbought reading for weeks during a major explosive bull market. The more explosive, the more the indicator will falsely be considered overbought.

Figure 5.1 is a good example of what I have been talking about. The market became overbought in mid-December and the market continued to skyrocket. On the other hand, the oversold conditions in February showed some promise as profitable trades.

The bottom line is that it is dangerous to trade just because the stochastics have moved to overbought or oversold. There needs to be some trigger to tell you when the buying has actually begun to dissipate. Otherwise, you will often be selling into a strong market with strong momentum. You know you are selling into a strong market when you sell an overbought market but you want to have a sign that the momentum is waning and the retracement is now going to occur. The crossover is that signal.

Let me show you how to really drill down on using crossovers as signals. I told you that this is not a profitable method to use mechanically, so be careful. However, there are times when you can use it to your advantage. I'm going to drill down to show you some nuances when you're using this technique. But don't make this a primary technique—it's dangerous!

TRADING SIGNALS FROM CROSSOVERS

Perhaps the most common use of stochastics is to give trading signals derived from the crossover of the slower moving line, the %D, by the faster moving line, the %K. The idea is that you sell the market when the %K crosses below the %D and buy when the %K crossed above the %D.

It is usually considered that the best signals come when the stochastic crossover occurs when the stochastics are above 80 percent or below 20 percent. These two levels give the most room for the signals to make money since the signal occurred when the market was overbought or oversold. Once again, I am not sure that this is so since selling into overbought bull markets is a dangerous game. Still, those are the usual rules.

Sometimes the %K will cross the %D when the %D is still climbing. This is called a *left-handed crossover* because the %K crosses over the %D on the left-hand side of the "hump" created by the %D. This will occur when the price changes sharply in the other direction. A *right-handed crossover* comes when the %K crosses over the %D on the right side of the "hump" of the %D. Figure 5.2 shows examples of both types of crossovers.

Most analysts prefer the right-handed crossover because they believe that it is a more stable market and that they are entering the market just after the turn in prices. A right-handed crossover will only occur when the market stabilizes first and then starts to drop. A right-handed crossover will also have the benefit of usually having both the %K and %D moving in the same direction when the crossover occurs. It is for this reason that many

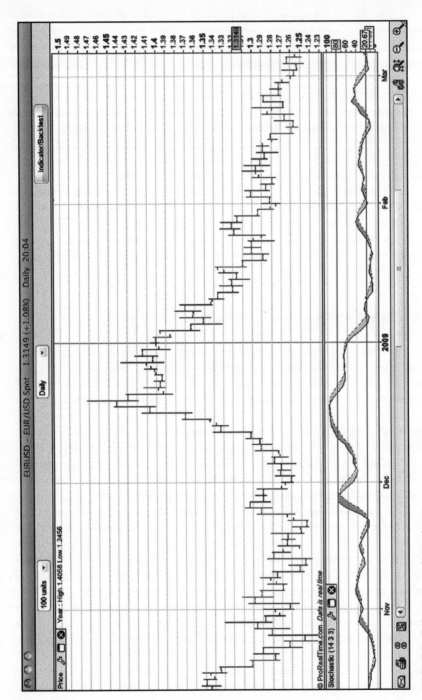

FIGURE 5.1 Euro with Stochastics

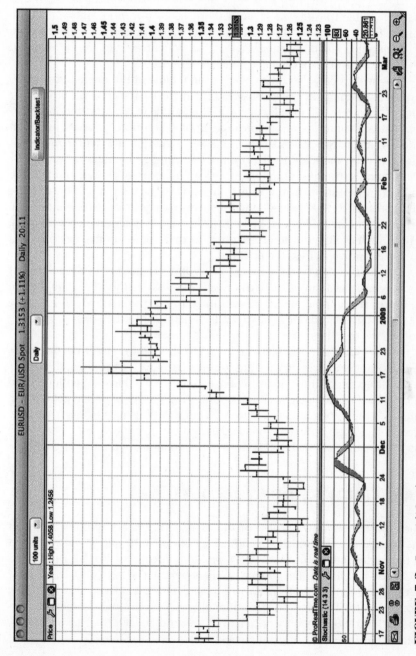

FIGURE 5.2 Euro with Stochastic Crossovers

investors prefer right-handed crossovers. It means that the momentum has changed significantly and that a trend has likely started.

However, the inventor of stochastics, George Lane, has suggested that it is acceptable to trade a left-handed crossover if it represents a resumption of the main trend. In particular, he suggests using it when a classic divergence (to be discussed next) has occurred and the left-handed crossover represents a resumption of the trend.

Stochastics can also cross over in the middle of the range between 20 and 80. They don't have to cross over only in the extremes of the stochastic range. Crossover will usually occur in the middle of a major trending market, that is, the market moves strongly in one direction, reverses, and then takes off again. Stochastics can give a sell signal during that retracement only to reverse back to the direction of the trend immediately after.

Generally, the idea is to buy or sell on the crossover and liquidate the trade on a crossover in the other direction. Obviously, this doesn't give much protection against sudden and strong moves in the wrong direction. As a result, many traders put in some protective stop based on recent price action, such as support and resistance, as disaster insurance against such a powerful move against the position.

Let me go back to the concept of trading crossovers in the middle of the range rather than at the extremes. I like this method because we are no longer using the concept of overbought and oversold, which I believe is very dangerous to our equity. But let's get back to the concept of using stochastics to tell us the momentum of the market.

We see that there is a strong trend in the market and that there has been a retracement. Now we want to use a crossover in the %K and %D only in the direction of the trend to enter a position. We have essentially used the stochastics to time the end of countertrend move and then get back in tune with the strong underlying trend. This way of using stochastics is very profitable. Please note that you need to find another way to set a protective stop. Typically, you will use the low of the countertrend move as the stop.

PROFITABILITY OF STOCHASTICS

There have been few studies of the profitability of using crossovers for trading signals. One study was done by Robert Colby and Thomas Meyers in their excellent book *The Encyclopedia of Technical Market Indicators* (McGraw-Hill, 1988). They focus on the stock market so they use the New York Stock Exchange (NYSE) Composite Index for their study, pulling monthly data. They tested period lengths of one through 24 over the period 1968 to 1986. My only criticism of the study is that they used monthly data rather than daily or even weekly data.

The results were very interesting.

The first rule they tested was a simple crossing of %K above or below %D. They optimized the results and found that every time period was a loser except at 21 months. Clearly, this method should be discarded.

The authors then tested a more robust rule of requiring that both the %K and %D had to be rising for a buy signal and dropping for a sell signal. This tends to mean that trades will be in the direction of the longer-term trend. What they found was that every period length was profitable except for the shortest lengths below six. Adding this new filter significantly improved the value of stochastics.

Obviously, many investors will not want to trade in a market using a monthly signal but even these people will want to consider using this as a powerful trend indicator to filter short-term trades. In other words, take short-term trades only in the direction of the long-term trend as identified by the long-term stochastic crossover. Note, too, that this monthly method can be used to time longer-term trades such as forex hedges for corporations.

They then tested the signals on weekly data over two different time periods. In this case, only signals around 50 weeks were profitable. Longer and shorter lengths were unprofitable. I think we can safely conclude that we should ignore this method.

Just because these tests were with stocks doesn't mean that they aren't important for us forex traders. But markets are markets. They are all traded by humans. Techniques in one financial arena very often work in other financial arenas.

Colby and Meyers also tested the concept of selling overbought markets and buying oversold markets and found that it was a huge loser. Let's just stick with following the trend.

WARNINGS

Because it is an oscillator, many traders look at the slope of the stochastics for an idea of the momentum of the market. They want to, say, buy when the stochastics are trending down but the momentum of *that* trend is waning. In effect, they don't want to wait for the crossover to get long. They want to get a jump on the stochastic crossover.

In other words, they will start to sell a market as the stochastics start to slow their advance. Take a close look at Figure 5.2. Notice that the %K will start to slow down its advance or decline while the %D is still moving at the same rate. Selling or buying when this happens will certainly give you a jump on the market change.

Not many people use the change in the slope to actually enter or exit the market. The main use is as another indicator to help predict the market's near-term direction.

Obviously, there are two main problems. First, there is the usual problem of selling into a major bull market. Second, occasionally the %K will reverse quickly and move again in the original direction. This is called a failure and I'll discuss this next.

THE BEST WAY TO MAKE MONEY USING STOCHASTICS

Now we get to the fun stuff. This is the real way to make money using stochastics. Let me first describe what divergences are.

One of the most popular modes of using stochastics is divergences. A *divergence* occurs when the price and stochastics diverge from following roughly the same path. In other words, if the price makes a new high but the stochastics don't, you have a divergence. If the stochastics make a new high but the price doesn't, you have a divergence. Divergences are mainly used to predict and trade a change in trend.

The typical divergence is when the price makes a new low but the stochastics don't or the price makes a new high and the stochastics don't. In other words, the momentum of the price is less strong than the price itself.

There are no specific entry and exit rules but I'll show you how to use stochastic divergences to create massive profits. We'll have to use other techniques to actually create the timing. We'll use stochastics to create the environment for making extra money.

I have studied this type of divergence and have found that divergences on the daily chart mean something different than divergences on the weekly chart. Divergences on the daily chart typically mean only that the market will likely have a short-term countertrend move. In general, I look for the market to change direction in one to five days (but most likely in two to three days) and have a one-to-five-day countertrend move (but most likely a two-to-three-day countertrend move).

A weekly divergence usually means that an intermediate-term trend change is about to happen. At the least, a weekly divergence means that there will be a significant countertrend move. I think that the size of the countertrend moves on the daily chart is not powerful enough to overcome the countertrend nature of the trade as well as the problem of deciding when the countertrend will begin.

On the other hand, the size of the projected weekly countertrend or new trend move was substantial and very tradable. There still remained the problem of being able to predict when the divergence would actually create the resulting change in trend. Nonetheless, a weekly divergence is far more tradable than a daily divergence.

It is a common belief that divergences do predict changes in trend, even if only a short countertrend move. But it is important to realize that you can't simply buy or sell when the divergence occurs. In virtually all cases, the market continues its trend for several more bars before succumbing to the power of the divergence. Many traders point out how great divergences called highs and lows but few, if any, argue that the divergence actually lasted for some period of time before the price turned direction. Let's look at a couple of examples.

In Figure 5.3, we see the price make a significant low about nine bars from the left (mid-December). The stochastics also make a low. However, six bars later, the market makes a new low close while the stochastics have not.

Note that I said a new low close, not a new low. That is because the relationship of the closes to the closes is the important factor, not the relationship of the lows to the lows. This is because stochastics are based on the closing price.

In this case, there was stochastic divergence but the price did not make a new significant low for three more bars. In our study, the divergence came three days in advance of the actual bottom. We then measure the distance from the actual bottom to the subsequent high to get an idea of the magnitude of the countertrend move. We measure this as a percent of the price of the underlying instrument to normalize the study over many futures contracts. For example, a move from 100-00 to 101-00 on the bonds would equal 1 percent. Obviously, this is not perfect, but it is still indicative of the magnitude when tested over 30 futures contracts.

Look at Figure 5.3 again and you will see several other divergences. The most significant one is the one about three-quarters through the chart. The market leaps to a new high with a very wide range bar but the stochastics do not make new highs. Eventually, a high is made and the market sells off but not before mounting a very strong rally.

In our study, we went back over one year of data on about 30 different commodities. These commodities were in various types of markets: bull, bear, and chop city. As a result, we get a good indication of the validity of using stochastic divergences.

First, we tested divergences on daily charts. We found 58 different divergences. They led a turn in the market by an average of 4.5 days with a standard deviation of 5.7. However, the mode was only 1 and the median

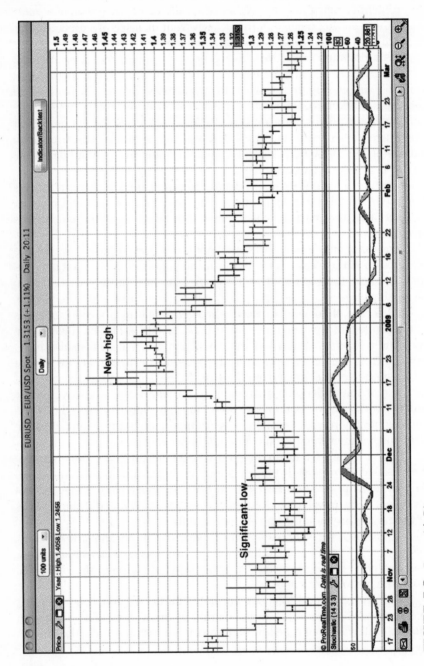

FIGURE 5.3 Euro with Divergences

was 2. The longest lead time was 22 days. As you can see, the lead time of daily divergences was random. This tends to reduce the value of daily divergences.

There were obviously 58 retracements from these 58 divergences. The average percentage retracement was 5.9 percent in a range of essentially 0 to a 21 percent retracement. The mode was 4 percent, and the median was 5 percent; the reliability of the retracement figures seems reasonable even though the standard deviation was 4.4 percent.

There were a lot more weekly divergences than daily divergences. We counted 124 during our sample period. They led turning points by an average of 2.8 weeks with a standard deviation of 3.4 weeks. The range was from calling the turning point exactly to 16 weeks in advance. Actually, the mode was calling the exact turning point. In other words, the most common occurrence of a weekly divergence was that week was the actual turning point, which is very interesting to me.

The average retracement of the 124 retracements was 15.3 percent with a standard deviation of 13.6 percent. Obviously, this is a far more powerful indicator of subsequent price movements than the daily divergences. The mode was, however, only 4 percent with a median of 11 percent though the maximum was 80 percent. Talk about a big move!

I'm about to say something that is astounding and perhaps heretical: It could be that divergences are simply illusions. Perhaps we are creating a pattern where none exists. For example, I could create a system that predicted a countertrend move soon after every day named Tuesday. Well, sure enough, this system will call 98 percent of every countertrend move within two weeks. In other words, only rarely will a market go two full weeks without retracing at least one day. Be aware of this potential problem. Having said that, I continue to use stochastic divergences on the daily and particularly on the weekly charts because I am making money using them.

A failure occurs when the %K changes direction, doesn't cross the %D, and reverses back to the original direction. Figure 5.4 shows two different failures. Arrows in the stochastic part of the chart show the failures. The first one occurs in early March when the %K actually drops but does not actually cross the %D. The second one occurs in late April. This is not a classic failure because it doesn't actually drop but it doesn't sharply slow and almost cross the %D. They often occur when there is a sharp retracement against the main trend but then an equally sharp resumption of the main trend.

The classic interpretation is that failure shows that the original trend will continue and that you should trade in that direction. In this case, that means jumping in the direction of the trend as soon as the %K resumes its original trend.

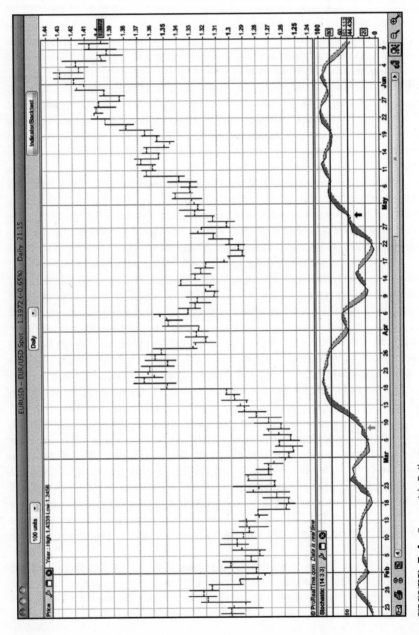

FIGURE 5.4 Euro with Failures

GO WITH THE TREND

I sometimes use stochastics as a mechanical trading system or as a trend indicator. The basic rule is to buy when the %K stochastic crosses above the 50 line and sell when it crosses below the 50 line. You are always in the market. I use this rule on both the weekly and daily bars, but mainly on the daily ones.

My experience is that the performance is similar to using any intermediate-term trend-following system. You will get chopped up during sideways price action but will make major profits when the market gets into a major trend.

Colby and Meyers tested this concept on NYSE Composite weekly data. (See the Appendix for more information.) They add one additional filter: The %K and the weekly closing price are above their previous week's level. Their results were that this was a profitable system using just about any length of parameter. This shows that the method is robust. However, profits were best near the 45-week level.

Colby and Meyers point out that only about 39 percent of trades were profitable. That is about what you would expect from any intermediate-term trading system.

The conclusion: This is a solid trend-following system that can be used on both weekly and daily data. The percentage of trades that are winners will be near 40 percent but the winners will be greater in size than the losers. One great advantage of this method is that it is free with every charting service.

HOW I USE STOCHASTICS

I pay attention to stochastics every day. I look for both daily and weekly divergences, in particular the weekly divergences. I look at the daily stochastics most often because that is the chart I mainly am living with day in and day out.

On the daily chart, I am mainly looking for divergences. Let's say that I see a divergence and I already have a position on and this position comes from a long-term technique like channel breakout. In this case, I would take off part of the position, perhaps one-quarter to one-half of the position. This should be a profit-taking exercise. My idea is that the market will setback for a few days. I will take some profits now and re-enter those liquidated positions should the market break to new highs.

Let's assume that I am right and the daily stochastic divergence actually causes the market to dip. Hopefully, that will cause the stochastics to cross down. I can then use an upside crossover to trigger a re-entry buy order. If the stochastics do not cross down, then I will rebuy the sold position when the market makes a new high.

Now, if I have no position but I am about to have a trade based on one of the core position methods, I want to follow the method and get long when the market breaks out. But I see that there is divergence developing, which suggests that the breakout will fail at least for several days.

I will go ahead and enter the buy order, but I will cut the position size in half or thereabouts. If I get into a position and there is the setback that I expect, then I can buy the rest of the position if the market makes a new high. On the other hand, I will only have a half-size position if the market continues higher. That situation is rare because daily stochastic divergence will usually cause a setback. So, basically, I use the daily stochastics to modify my already existing trading methods.

Weekly stochastics are far more powerful than daily ones since they lead to either a significant retracement or a major trend change. My trading strategy here is to use them the same way I described using the daily stochastics, but I will also become aggressive at finding an entry point in the direction that the divergence is predicting. For example, let's assume that the market is moving higher but develops a bearish stochastic divergence. That would predict at least a strong retracement that is big enough to make a nice profit.

If I am long, I will look for any excuse to exit the long position. If I have no position, I will look for any excuse to get short. This is more aggressive than the techniques outlined in earlier chapters.

By "any excuse" I mean that I will take any technique outlined in this book and jump on the short side with little or no confirmation. For example, the market is heading higher but a divergence appears. I'll get short if I see something like a reversal bar down on the daily chart. It doesn't have to be much of a signal to get me short. I'll also use that signal to exit my position trades from techniques such as the Conqueror or trend analysis.

INTERVIEW WITH GEORGE LANE

I was fortunate to get a phone interview with the inventor of stochastics, George Lane. He was quite old at the time and has since died. He was a great character. He was mainly a trader of Standard & Poor's (S&P) futures, but his comments apply to forex trading.

The interview is word for word, so some of the grammar is fractured and there is some stumbling that is natural in spoken English.

Author: *Are stochastics your primary form of analysis of the market?*

George Lane: Oh, yes. It beats everything else I've discovered or tried. It's damn near infallible, once you get to know how to use it.

A: *Do you use it mainly as a trend indicator or overbought/oversold or crossovers or what?*

GL: I'm a short-term trader. We trade about three or four times a day. I use it to signal buys at the bottom. I day trade S&P's.

A: *Do you use crossovers to signal the buys?*

GL: Why don't we take out the word "crossover" out of it? The crossover happens but that isn't the signal. The signal is divergence.

A: *Does the divergence have to be in overbought or oversold territory or can it be anywhere on the chart?*

GL: Most of the time it will be in the overbought/oversold territory. Those are the safest. We take some in the midrange.

A: *When you see a divergence, will you then use a crossover to signal an entry?*

GL: No, just the divergence.

A: *So, you will buy or sell just as soon as you see the divergence?*

GL: You have to combine old-fashioned charting with stochastics and it's damn near infallible.

A: *So let me get this straight. I'm seeing a divergence on the downside. Will you then be looking for a reversal bar or breakout above a previous high after you get the divergence?*

GL: Yes, or at the same time. Stochastics is a hair early. It's a leading indicator. A lot of times you will get your stochastic divergence and then one or two bars later, you will get your chart signal.

A: *Do you find that is the case on dailies and weeklies as well as on shorter-term bars?*

GL: Absolutely. I use exactly the same technique on long term as I do on short term.

A: *Do you feel that the crossover of the 50 percent level is of any significance?*

GL: No. Once it breaks the 50 percent, I know I'm right. I don't put much weight on it.

A: *Do you ever look at right-handed or left-handed crossovers?*

GL: Yes. Say the market comes down and makes a great big double bottom. At the first bottom, you're going to have a left-handed crossover. That tells you "wait." You're going to get a right-handed crossover and that's going to be a better signal. So you wait for the second bottom of the double bottom, get the right-handed crossover, and then you go.

A: *So the right-handed crossover is more significant.*

GL: It is the important one, yes, sir.

A: *Some people say that when the stochastics first cross 80 percent that is a good time to buy and that is a good trend signal.*

GL: That's Jake Bernstein's interpretation. He discovered, and we have been teaching for 47-some years, that sometimes stochastics goes on up to the top and the market keeps on going. In other words, there's just so damn much momentum to it that it just keeps on going. Stochastics, when it gets up around 100, can't do anything so it just bobbles along the ceiling. That kind of thing happens and they are marvelous.

So when it gets up around 75, he's a buyer. If I bought one down near the bottom, I can buy another one up there but I have a little trouble buying the first one up there.

A: *What about the formation you call a knee or a shoulder or failure? Do you see that very often and do you find it worthwhile?*

GL: Yes, sir, it happens. It doesn't happen very often but it does happen.

You see, if the market comes down and gives me a left-handed crossover . . . I'm going to wait for the right-handed crossover. But then K rallies and then comes back and kisses D and then starts to go back up again. Now I have a convergence in K only. So I jump on it and go. It means that we might not get that right-handed crossover because I got a legitimate right-handed crossover in K.

You take a divergence in K or D or both. So if you don't get your divergence in D but do get it in K, go!

A: *Let's say you have entered a position on a divergence. How do you set your protective stop loss?*

GL: Two clicks below the lowest of the two previous lows.

A: *Where did the name "stochastics" come from?*

GL: Stochastics is an advanced form of statistics. In statistics, every so often they run across a situation that has so much data that they have to use other ways of studying. I sat next to a stochastics engineer flying out to San Francisco one time. He explained it to me as an advanced level of statistics. He was going out to redesign the lenses of the Hubble telescope because the data of all the stars in the sky was so enormous that they had to change things a little bit. That's a good illustration of where they use it.

A: *Who came up with the name "stochastics"?*

GL: Stochastics is that discipline in statistics or engineering that they use. Percent deviation, or %D, is the name of the indicator. Percent deviation from normal.

A: *That's %D. Where does %K come from?*

GL: Somebody in the pit one day said that they wish they had a leading indicator for this darn thing. I looked and it was right there in our calculation so I named it after my middle name, Kelly!

After we used it for a few years, Computrac gleamed onto it in their committee of 30 and suggested they use it. When they got it all programmed and ready to use, Tim Slater asked them what are they going to call it, and the guy said that he thought it was a stochastic-type thing. So they called it stochastics.

It's not a stochastic-type indicator at all but it got that name and it hung on. I didn't have any control.

A: *What is the relationship of stochastics with Larry Williams's %R?*

GL: The first thing we discovered was %R. We discovered that in 1948.

%R is stochastics upside down. We used it for a while. When you make a signal at the top, you buy and when you make a signal on the bottom, you sell it. So we turned it right-side up to make it more practical. We had written some stuff on it. I think that one of Larry's friends came to one of our seminars and took it home and Larry thought it was a good thing and published it and put his name on it.

A: *Is stochastics a better oscillator than a rate of change or RSI?*

GL: Welles Wilder's RSI is a damned good indicator. It's nothing but a closing price chart. If you take off the open, high, and low and make a chart with just the close, you're going to get the same type of pattern that you get with RSI. It will show the divergences and things like that. So a closing price chart was used early in my experience. It was a good indicator.

Welles Wilder's RSI is a complicated way of figuring that. It's a damned good indicator but it's a one-line indicator and it fails maybe once every 20 times to give you a good clean signal. Whereas stochastics just damn near never fails.

We used RSI along with stochastics for several years but we finally came to the conclusion that we don't need two oscillators so we just quit using RSI because we don't need it.

I used volume instead of RSI.

A: *How do you use volume?*

GL: Volume is a very standard thing. We've been teaching that for 45 to 50 years.

A: *What term stochastics do you use? Most chart services use either 9 or 14 days.*

GL: Well, a charting service has to have them all the same because they use a computer to generate the charts.

What you do is look at the chart. Let's say you are looking at dailies. You look over a few days and locate the cycle. The cycle that you see, not necessarily the cycle that the guy in the next desk sees. The rule is, in analysis, when you are working on an indicator and there is a moving average in the indicator (to smooth or optimize it), the input data for that indicator will be 50 percent of the cycle that you are trading. So you just look at the charts and find the cycle. There is usually a cycle that is fairly common. It may vary a little bit but it is fairly repetitive. You take half the number of bars of the cycle and that is the input data for the stochastics. Now you are designing the stochastics to fit the cycle that you see. Therefore, that will be the most successful for you.

A: *What does the cycle length have to do with anything?*

GL: The rule is in the analysis of oscillators, whenever you are developing an oscillator of any kind, the input data to calculate that oscillator is going to be 50 percent of the cycle you are trading. Then you will have the most optimum oscillator.

A: *Is there any particular reason why that should be? Why not the full cycle?*

GL: You've got moving averages in your oscillator to smooth it. Any time you use a moving average, like the 10-day moving average, you are going to be five days behind the last trade. So you take the input data that shows your last trade, which, on a 30-day oscillator will be 15 days back. So that seems to be the most successful.

I've researched that for years and I haven't changed it.

A: *So each commodity will have a different length for calculating the stochastic?*

GL: This makes stochastics a little more successful and a little more reliable than just arbitrarily picking a number.

A: *In general, would you say that the chart services have se-lected a good average at about 14 days input?*

GL: I think that looking at the daily charts 14 or 15 is a pretty good average. It's usually a 30-day cycle.

I used to trade the S&P's a few years ago and they had a 28-day cycle. It lasted for four or five years. Now, of course, with the volatility that the S&P's are in now, the cycle has shrunk to less than 28 days.

We are getting very volatile markets. We are at the end of a 60- or 70-year cycle and this is the blow-off period and things are getting wild, as you know.

A: *Who invented stochastics?*

GL: I did.

A: *When was that?*

GL: We started on this in about 1948.

A: *How did you come up with the concept?*

GL: Well, there [were] six of us and we traded on the MidAmer-ica Commodity Exchange. Every night we would go over to Investment Educators' office. We were trying every damn fool thing we could think of. We were using the alphabet. We had reduced everything to percentage because then the range would be from 0 to 100 and it would make the oscilla-tor more practical.

We went through the alphabet I think twice.

We had an old Czechoslovakian immigrant there who was a friend of one of the Polish boys that was kind of help-ing me. He told us, in his broken English, about a formula that they used in Czechoslovakia to figure out how much limestone to put in the steel mix when they were melting iron and stuff to make steel. We took that stupid formula of his and readjusted it and played with it and that was the tip-off for what is now stochastics!

We were desperate. We were grasping at straws because we knew that there was something out there but we just couldn't find it.

A: *Who else was involved?*

GL: There were about four or five people helping me or doing the same thing. They were all Polish people. Gosh, I don't even remember their names anymore. I know one of them went over to the Chicago Board of Trade and got to be a big player. I remember one day he had a big position and he wanted to go and visit his girlfriend up in Michigan and told a buddy of his to get him out of his position. His buddy forgot to get him out and the market opened the next day and went straight down for three days and he got wiped out! So he quit and went back to teaching! He lost $360,000 in just two or three days. I felt so sorry for him.

A: *When was that?*

GL: Oh, that was in 1948 or 1949.

A: *So that was real money then!*

GL: Yeah, that was huge money! And he was a damned good trader. He was using stochastics very well.

A: *What did you call stochastics back then, %D?*

GL: As soon as Computrac came out with their software and called it stochastics, I had no choice but to call it stochastics. But I called it %D until Computrac gave it a name.

The most popular oscillators are stochastics, RSI, and MACD. RSI is damn near as good as stochastics except that it is a one-line indicator and it is much easier with stochastics because it has two lines and it can give you two signals to do something. MACD is a very fine oscillator but it's quite late. By the time you get signals to do something with MACD, it's already gone.

Those are the three most popular. I think that Computrac did some research and asked about 9,000 of their members and I think that stochastics was number one and RSI was 30 points behind that and then MACD was 50 points behind that in popularity.

Do you know that every mutual fund is using stochastics? I hear from some of them every once in a while. They call me up and thank me for inventing this marvelous indicator and they use it all the time.

I think that it is the most universally used because it is in every software program.

A: *Any other comments you can pass on to us?*

GL: We've just developed the methodology of trading. We trade three-minute bars on the Swiss franc and the S&P and stuff like that. We use stochastics and volume and normal charting techniques and patterns and we find that those three things together are almost awesome. They will sometimes go two or three weeks without a loss.

A: *Doing day trades?*

GL: We trade an average of four times a day. I traded the one-minute bars one day and it gives you a lot more signals. I think I had 38 trades.

I think I made money. I know the broker did.

    A: *I know one thing and that is that the broker always wins!*

GL: Isn't that wonderful! When you win, he wins. When you lose, he wins.

    A: *Well, George, now I know why you were in the brokerage business for so long!*

THE BOTTOM LINE

Stochastics are an interesting technique. It is amazing that they are so popular yet are so misused. I think that George Lane and I have shown you how to use them properly and profitably!

CHAPTER 6

Pattern Recognition

To a certain extent, all analysis is pattern recognition. In technical analysis, things such as head and shoulders is a pattern. Every technique that I have taught you previously is the recognition of patterns and then acting on those patterns. Even fundamental analysis is pattern recognition. Money supply expansion is a pattern that leads us to act.

However, pattern recognition usually refers only to short-term patterns of price action and then acting on that. For example, the market closes higher then lower then higher. What does the market do the following day? That would be a short-term pattern.

I want to highlight several profitable price patterns that you can use to create daily profits. I'm going to show you my spin on two classics, inside days and reversal days, and show you a unique concept called riding the rejection rule, or RRR.

All of the core techniques that I have discussed so far have focused on position trades (trades we hope to hold for days and weeks). The patterns that I describe in this chapter are basically short-term patterns (trades we will hold for 24 hours or less).

INSIDE DAYS

The first pattern is called an *inside day*. This pattern is a classic pattern that has been around for decades. It's like a mini version of the channel breakout.

Let's first take a look at what an inside day is. In Figure 6.1, I've placed three arrows on the chart. Let's start with the one on the left side of the chart. The arrow is pointing to March 3. This is a good example of an inside day. An *inside day* is any day that has its whole range inside the range of the previous day. In other words, the high of the inside day is lower than the high of the previous day and the low of the inside day is higher than the low of the previous day. Take a look at March 3. Note that its high is much lower than the high of the previous day and the low is modestly higher than the previous day's low. The whole range of March 3 is within the range of the previous day. Thus, it is an inside day.

Take a look at the other two days with arrows pointing to them. The arrows are pointing at inside days. In all cases, the range of the inside day is inside the range of the previous day. That makes it pretty easy to spot on a chart.

An inside day is a day of balance. It is a day when the bulls and bears have fought to a draw. Neither side has enough power to push the market in any direction with any force. In fact, the bulls don't even have enough power to push the market above the high of the previous day and the bears don't have the power to push the market below the low of the previous day. Balance! (Inside days are often short-term turning points, but that's a story for another time.)

What we want to do is to follow whoever wins the battle. We want to get long if the bulls win and go short if the bears win. We want to go with the power flow.

We first identify which days are inside days. We have to wait until the end of the day before we know that. We then place a buy stop order just above the high of the inside day and place a sell stop order just under the low of the inside day. Your protective stop order for the long position, if filled on the long side, places a protective stop just under the low of the inside day. If filled on the short position, then place a protective stop just above the high of the inside day. If your trading platform allows you to place contingent stop orders then put in the protective stops when you put in your original entry orders. Otherwise, enter the protective orders after you get filled on the entry order.

Now let's follow what happens when we get filled. Let's use the trade on March 4 as an example. In this case, the market opens near the low end of the inside day of March 3 and then moves higher until it finally moves above the high of the inside day where it triggers a buy order. We are now long. Put in a protective stop at just below the low of the inside day (if you have not put it in when you entered the original entry order).

Let's stop for a minute and consider where our orders are. We are long and have a protective stop order just under the low of the inside day. We also still have an order to go short on a break of the low of the inside

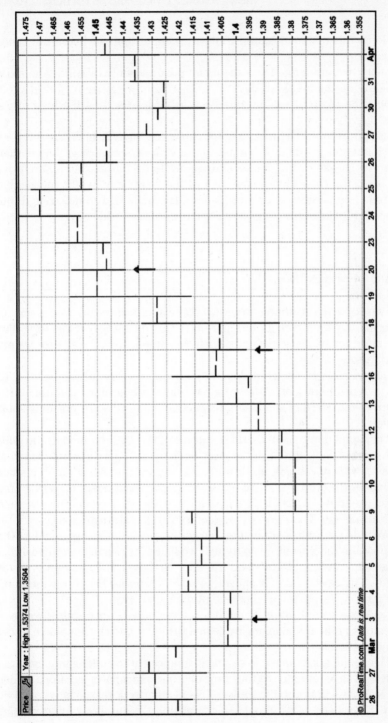

FIGURE 6.1 Euro with Inside Days Marked

day. Keep this in mind because it plays an important role in our upcoming discussion.

Okay, we are long. The exit of the position will always be the close of trading on the breakout day. So, in this case, we make a modest profit because the close of trading turns out to be higher than the high of the inside day.

Let's now look at a losing trade. Go over to March 20 in Figure 6.1. Here we see another inside day. We put in our orders just as described earlier. The price breaks to the upside and we get long. Unfortunately, the price sags back and closes below the high of the inside day, which means that the trade is a modest loser. In this case, the bulls had some strength but not enough to keep the price above the high of the inside day.

DOUBLE WHAMMY

Now we come to the double whammy. Take a look at the arrow pointing to the inside day on March 17 in Figure 6.1. This day is very interesting. Pay close attention because this will get a little complicated. Recall how we put in the various orders.

In this case, the price dropped and broke the low of the inside day. That gets us short. Don't forget that we have a buy order just above the high of the inside day and also a protective stop order for our new short position.

The bears don't maintain their control of the market. In fact, the bulls come roaring back and push the price back up through the whole range of the inside day and break up through the high of the inside day. This last fact causes the stop loss to be triggered on the short position to ring up a loss on the trade. But it also triggers a buy order that we put in at the end of the inside day. This entry order gets triggered and we get long.

We hold the long position until the end of the day when we liquidate the long position for a profit. Even though we had a loss on the initial position, we gained a profit on the second trade for slightly less than breakeven for the day. This type of day is called a *double whammy* because we end up trading twice during the day instead of the usual once.

I call the second trade of the day a *lemonade trade* because we took the lemons of the initial losing trade and turned it into the lemonade of the second profitable trade.

This lemonade concept is a critical component to making money in the markets. It is an attempt to turn unprofitable trades into profitable trades or at least less unprofitable trades. This is a concept that is never spoken about. Everybody talks about the initial trade. Many books and articles have been written about buy and sell signals. Virtually every book is on how to use a system to create profitable trading. But nobody talks about what to do after the original trade is over. In particular, nobody tells you what to do when the trade fails.

A very old trading precept says that a failed signal is a signal. So every trade that is a losing trade might be setting up a winning trade. Take a look at every technique you are using and see if it is profitable for you to reverse your position when you get stopped out of a trade. So, for example, suppose you are short using the super-duper widget system and you get stopped out. What would happen if you were to reverse your position to the long side? And perhaps hang on just until the end of the day? I'll bet you have a new profitable system!

In this case, we are reversing our position whenever we get stopped out using inside days. A stopped-out inside day trade is always a double whammy.

Inside days tend to be profitable in about 55 percent of trades with the average winning trade much larger than the average losing trade. But lemonade trades are profitable at a rate of about 70 to 75 percent and the average winning trade is still much larger than the average losing trade.

More conservative traders may even want to trade only the lemonade trade and skip the initial trade. You'll only be able to identify the potential for a lemonade trade after you see the price break one end of the inside day's range. You then place an entry order in on the opposite side of the inside day's range. So, for example, put in a buy order once you see the price break down through the low of the inside day.

You will have far fewer trades if you only trade the lemonade trade but you will have a much higher percentage of winning trades. Lemonade trades account for almost 50 percent of the total profits from trading inside days. I trade both the initial trade and the lemonade trade because I am willing to take the additional psychological heat in return for the additional profits.

MULTIUNIT TACTIC

There is another way that we can enhance the profitability of inside days. I call it the multiunit tactic. I've been writing about this since my book on spread trading in 1983.

So far, in this book, we have talked about every technique assuming that we are going to enter a position with only one contract. But, of course, there is no reason to assume that we have to trade only one contract for every position. Yes, a person with limited funds in their account will only be able to trade one contract if they are using proper risk management techniques (see Chapter 7 for more information). But most traders will be able to put on two or more contracts when they enter a position. You can use the multiunit technique as long as you can enter two or more contracts.

Virtually all written material, including this book, assumes that you will only have one contract on. Even if more contracts are assumed, it is assumed that the entry and exit are the same for both positions. But why should each contract have the same tactic? Why not change it up a little?

In this case, let's assume that we have enough money in our account to buy or sell two contracts. Let's say that we get a buy signal using the inside day technique. We would buy two contracts at that point. But instead of holding both positions until the close of trading, which is the standard exit, we liquidate one of the two contracts when there is a 20-pip profit. We carry the second position to the end of the trading day just as described in the standard rules for this method. Does the multiunit tactic enhance profits? Yes!

Let's look at the three trades in Figure 6.1. On the first trade, on the left, we make more money because we take off one of the two positions near the high of the day and then the price sags back down to the close. We enhanced profits slightly here.

Let's take a look at the double whammy day in the middle. Here, we short two contracts and take profits on one of them quickly. The market then reverses and moves up through the high of the inside day. This gets us long but only on one contract since we have already eliminated one of our contracts. So our losing trade is on one of the two contracts but we have made money on the first contract. We then kick in the lemonade trade on one contract, which gives us a nice profit. The net result of these trades is that we end up about breakeven for the day!

The final trade is the losing trade on the right side of the chart. Here, we get long two contracts when the price penetrates the high of the inside day. We quickly take profits of 20 pips on one contract and then carry the second contract to the close of trading for a loss. The bottom line is that the profit on the first contract essentially covers the loss on the second contract.

The multiunit tactic enhanced the profit of each trade in these common examples. Every so often we will get into a position and then the market immediately turns around and you get stopped out with twice the size. That will hurt, but it will be a rare occurrence.

And, of course, you will kick yourself when you take off one contract and the trade would have made a ton of money. This is really the cost of the multiunit tactic. You will occasionally miss a big trade with two contracts but the multiunit tactic will enhance your profits most of the time for a net gain.

REVERSAL DAYS

My second pattern recognition method is another classic: reversal days. This is another technique that has been around for decades. And, once again, I'll provide some enhancements for it.

The reversal day concept comes from the idea that it is important to watch for situations when the market starts off in one direction on a given day but then turns around and moves sharply in the other direction.

Let's take a look at a typical Reversal Day. Figure 6.2 shows four different reversal days marked with arrows. Let's take a look at the first one.

A Reversal Day occurs when a pair makes a lower low than the previous day and closes higher. On the bear side, a Reversal Day is a day where the market makes a higher high than the previous day and closes lower. The first arrow on the left is pointing to a bullish Reversal Day. You can see that it made a lower low than the previous day but closed higher on the day. Now, take a look at the day before the inside day. On this day, the market opened then traded up to the highs, showing that the bulls were in control of the market early in the day. But the market closed near its lows, showing that the bears had taken control of the market. This bearish control continues at the beginning of the inside day on February 20. The market moves lower on a continuation of the bearish price action of the February 19.

But then the bulls start to take control. They come in with enough power that they are able to move above the previous day's close and close higher for the day. In fact, they were so powerful that they were able to even break above the high of February 19, though they weren't able to maintain that level. Still, it took a lot of buying power for the bulls to be able to turn the tide of the bears from that day and bull the market higher.

We must always pay attention to markets that do unusual things. In this case, the bulls were able to reverse the trend of the previous day and move the market higher.

Our trading strategy is to buy at the close of trading of the inside day and hold the position until the close of trading the next day. Our protective stop loss is just below the low of the inside day. We will also lemonade that stop loss and go short if we get stopped out. The lemonade trade will still be liquidated on the close of the day following the inside day. So, in this case, the market moves somewhat higher after we enter the long position and we make a little money.

There is one filter for this method. I like to take trades in the direction of the trend. In this case, the short-term trend was higher so I took the trade. I don't put on reversal days against the trend. What this means is that the reversal day is actually signaling that the short-term correction against

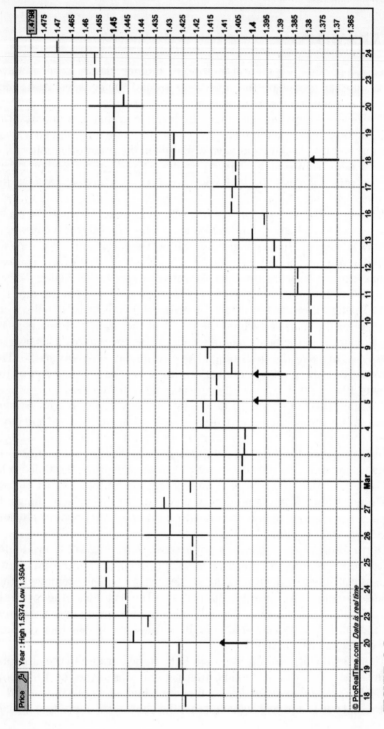

FIGURE 6.2 Euro with Reversal Days Marked

the main trend is over and that the true underlying trend has reasserted itself. We are getting back in tune with the market. We are not fighting the market.

The first trade on the chart was a resumption of the bull trend that had been in force prior to the downward action that occurred on the February 19 and early on the February 20. And, as a result, we had a modest winner.

Let's go to the 25th of February and we see a large downward pointing reversal day. Here, the market makes a higher high than the previous day but closes lower on the day. This is an interesting bar. We had been in a bull market to that point. Clearly, this is a powerful down day and the high of the day failed to make a new high on the swing so we get two pieces of evidence that the trend is turning down at that point. We don't know that it will be much of a down trend but at least we know that the market is heading lower over the short run. So we take that bearish reversal day trade on February 25 but it turns into a modest loser the next day.

Note that the day that we have a modest loser is also a reversal day to the upside. We don't take that trade because, at that point, we are now considering that we are in a bear mode and so we will only take bearish reversal day trades.

The next bearish reversal day is March 5. Once again, we make a higher high but close lower on the day. We go short on the close of the day with a protective stop at the high of the day. In fact, we get stopped out and we also get long on a lemonade trade that also fails! Our original reversal day trade would have been profitable if we did not have a protective stop in, but you can't have everything.

Notice that the market ended up closing lower on the day after making a higher high than the previous day. Once again, we have a reversal day created on March 6. Fortunately, the market follows the normal pattern and collapses, creating a huge profit for us. That takes the sting out of the previous day!

The next reversal day is the very lowest bar on the chart: March 11. Go back over your charts and you will often see that significant highs and lows are actually reversal days. We don't take this trade because we still believe that it is a bear market and we only take trades in the direction of the market. Too bad, it would have been a profitable trade. By the way, it is profitable to take all reversal bars regardless of whether they are congruent with the trend. However, you don't get much more total profit and you have to suffer through a lot more losing trades, thus making it psychologically more difficult to stick to the system.

At the end of trading on March 18, we can see clearly that the short-term trend has switched to bullish. That day was a powerful day because it showed that the trend had changed. It is also a reversal day so we get long with a protective stop just under the low of the day. Bingo! Another nice profit as the power of the big reversal day carries through and moves the market much higher.

This sample of trades shows every circumstance that you will encounter in trading reversal bars. Most trades will be winners. Some will be losers. You will be stopped out only rarely and thus will not be putting on many lemonade trades. In this chapter, I showed such a trade but it will only happen rarely. Most trades are small winners or small losers with the occasional big winner putting you into the profit column for the year.

You can also use the reversal days technique as a trend indicator. Generally speaking, reversal days move in the direction of the dominant trend. In this chapter, we had several downward pointing reversal days during the late February/early March period and, in fact, the market was generally heading lower. We switched to mainly upward pointing reversal days starting with the low bar on the chart on March 11 and going forward. This was a period of bullish reversal days and a bull market in the price.

I also use the reversal bars technique to get me into longer-term position trades. Let's say that you missed your long-term position entry based on the techniques discussed previously. Those methods are nearly all breakout trend-following techniques of some type. Or, perhaps, you are already in a market and want to add to your position. For whatever reason, reversal days are a great way to enter a longer-term position.

One reason why reversal days are so great is that they get you into a trending market at the end of a countertrend move. For example, the market has been moving higher but sets back for several days. This is usually when the reversal day kicks in as a signal. It usually triggers after a short-term correction in a market. You are therefore getting into a market at a very advantageous point. You can then use some other exit strategy to protect the position. For example, use a three-bar low from trend analysis as the protective stop when you enter a position using reversal bars.

Notice that every single losing trade would have been mitigated by using the multiunit tactic. You would have been able to create a small profit on every trade even before moving to a loss or getting stopped out.

One way to modify the original trade idea is not to carry the trade to the close of the following day but to simply take a quick 20- to 40-pip profit after entering the trade. You are surfing the initial momentum of the trade and taking a quick profit. You are taking the momentum that the reversal bar is identifying and riding that to a profit. You are not assuming that the momentum runs until the end of the day. You are assuming that you should bail out right away.

Note that almost all your trades will be winners using the multiunit tactic here because the momentum of the reversal bar creates its own profits. Losses will be uncommon and getting stopped out will be rare. However, note that your losses will likely be larger than your winners and getting stopped out will eliminate a lot of winning trade profits. The pattern of the multiunit tactic has lots of little winners and a few larger losses. But the bottom line is that you will make money using this technique.

Adding the multiunit tactic to your options will also enhance the total profits of reversal bars over a long period of time. You are effectively using the reversal bars to diversify through time. You are using it to take quick profits and daily profits. What this means is that you are using the power to create profits in two time frames. This diversification will actually reduce the risk you take while enhancing profits at the same time. The interaction between the two uses of the reversal bar creates additional profits with less risk.

RIDING THE REJECTION RULE

The third pattern-recognition technique is a unique method I call riding the rejection rule, or RRR. Read about the rejection rule in Chapter 3 on channel breakouts if you don't remember the rejection rule. I am going to show you how to turn a losing trade, triggered by the rejection rule, into a profitable trade. In effect, this method is another of our lemonade trades because we take a losing trade and turn it into either a profitable trade, or at least less of a loss. You can also use RRR as a stand-alone technique to make money!

The basic concept of this technique came from my reading of Linda Bradford Raschke and Larry Connor's book *Street Smart Trading* (M. Gordon Publishing Group, 1996). They outlined a technique called Turtle Soup. That was the genesis of RRR.

Raschke and Connor noticed that markets often fail to follow through when they break through levels that traders focus on. One of the most important levels was the 20-day high and low. As I discussed in Chapter 3, this was the level that Richard Donchian outlined in his four-week rule (4WR). The 4WR was then adapted by the Turtles (a group of traders, only some of whom have ever been named). Raschke and Connors felt that the market would often go to these breakout levels and fail. The Turtle modifications didn't really address this issue.

So Raschke and Connors thought that they should trade the failed breakouts. Remember that I told you that a failed signal is a signal. RRR is a technique for finding failed signals and then jumping on them. We are looking for a breakout that fails and then profiting from that failure. The discussion thus far has been on the 20-day breakout but I prefer to use RRR on the 55-day breakout used in our channel breakout technique. I do this for several reasons. I am looking to enter trades on a break of the 55-day

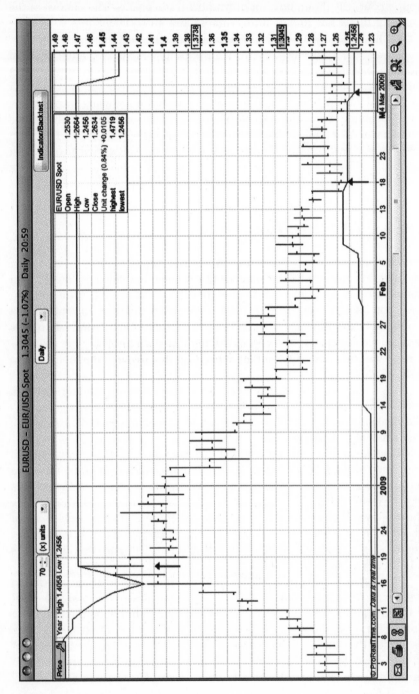

FIGURE 6.3 Euro with RRR Marked

high or low so I am more aware of the 55-day breakouts. I find that 55-day breakouts are more significant so they yield higher profits than the 20-day breakouts. That also means that false breakouts are more significant. We expect that the market will follow through when we make a 55-day break-out. It is very significant if that fails. So I expect that failed signal here to be more powerful than on the 20-day breakouts.

This is not to say that using RRR on 20-day breakouts won't work. It will. But the percentage of winning trades will be lower. Still, I recommend that you use RRR on both the 20- and the 55-day breakouts. More conserva-tive traders should consider only using RRR on the 55-day breakouts. Let's look at the rules of RRR. Let's take a look at some examples. Once again, I've selected a sample time period that gives us a good cross-selection of winning and losing trades. In Figure 6.3, there is a black arrow on the left side of the chart. The solid black line shows the 55-day high and low.

You can see that the market broke out of the 55-day high on the day before the day with the arrow. But the market gets rejected the next day on a reversal day no less! Our entry rule is to sell (or buy) whenever we are stopped out of our entry trades using the channel breakout technique. Our protective stop is the other end of our entry bar. We exit the trade at the close of trading.

So, in this first trade, we enter on the close of trading on the bar with the arrow. Our protective stop is the high of the bar. The next day, the market continues the plunge that started on the arrowed day. We exit on the close for a large profit.

Let's go over to the bar on February 18. The rejection rule kicks in when the price closes above the breakout level. We get long on the close with a protective stop at the low of the bar. Actually, note that our protec-tive stop is really just an entry back into the regular channel breakout.

THE BOTTOM LINE

These three patterns—inside days, reversal days, and riding the rejection rule—are the foundation of a day trading program that can grind out profits week in and week out. I like them because I can put them on each day no matter what the trend is and make money each week. I view them as my equivalent of W-2 income. These techniques don't hit home runs, but they hit single after single. That adds up by the end of the year.

In addition, the multiunit tactic gives us significantly more flexibility in our buying and selling decisions. We can fine-tune our tactics on a much higher level after adding this method.

CHAPTER 7

Risk Management

R isk management is the second most important factor in trading success. Psychology reigns supreme because you need to have a correct psychology to make sure you can execute proper risk management, but you must control the risk in your account if you want to control the reward in your account. You will not have any idea of how successful you can be without knowing how *unsuccessful* you can be. Lacking proper risk management makes you a gambler, not a speculator. You are out of control of your investments when you don't use proper risk management.

STOPPING BAD RISK MANAGEMENT

Bad risk management can create stress that leads to bad trading. I have seen many traders be both financially and psychologically debilitated by a large loss or a string of losses. How many times have you seen people capitulate after fighting the market by being long and a bear market relentlessly kills their equity?

Once that bad risk management blows our mind, we are lost as traders. We will start to do self-destructive things as "double up to catch up." We will look to punish a market to make up for our losses. Or we will hesitate and not put on trades we should put on.

You can have the greatest method in the world but it will be a failure if you don't control your risk. All methods take losses. But what if those losses cause you to be wiped out? You won't have the money power to come back to create all those glorious profits that the greatest method will create.

Bad risk management is perhaps the most common reason for failure as a forex trader. People tend to overtrade and put on bigger positions than their equity can handle. They come into forex trading because of some hype and think they can make a million dollars in the first month. They think that all they have to do is follow the new system they bought and they can't go wrong. They put on a few trades that are way too big for their small equity and the first few trades go south and they are financially crippled. They are also likely mentally crippled and think that it is impossible for anyone to make money in forex.

The hyped system may or may not be garbage. These traders will never know, because they got blown out so quickly, that they never really gave the system a real chance to succeed.

As you can see, psychology and risk management complement and support each other. We always want to be cool, calm, and collected when we trade and that won't be possible if we are overtrading or have on positions that are too large or if we have losses that are too large for our mind. We need to remain rational at all times when we trade. The stakes are too high to not do otherwise.

How do you feel when you take a large loss? I thought so. I don't feel good either. So it is important that we keep our losses to trivial levels. We want to have losses so small that we can't remember them the following day. They should be so trivial that we hardly notice them and they certainly don't cause us any mental pain.

Capital preservation is more important than capital appreciation. I have seen so many traders come to me for training after they have lost 50 percent of their money. Stop and think about this for a minute. They need to now double their money just to get back to breakeven! That's not easy. They could get back to breakeven in just one trade if they were down only a few percent.

And think about the psychology of the traders who have lost 50 percent of their funds? Do you think they are approaching the market in a cool, calm manner? Do you think their minds are blown? What chances do you give them to double their money?

Risk management can take a good system and make it a bad one. Bad risk management will destroy a good system.

Good risk management is more important than having a good system. Bad risk management can turn a profitable system into an unprofitable system, but not vice versa.

Let's play a game. Let's assume that you are going to flip a coin. Let's further assume that you have $100 and you are going to flip the coin 1,000 times. This is a totally fair game. All we are going to do is to change the size of the bet.

First, let's assume that we bet $10 on every flip of the coin. That's 10 percent of our bankroll of $100. What are the chances that we will get wiped out sometime during our 1,000 coin flips? Turns out that we have over a 90 percent chance of getting wiped out. The reason is that all we need is a net of 10 losing trades and we are wiped out. And there is over a 90 percent chance that we will get that condition sometime during those 1,000 flips.

Now, let's only bet $1 on each flip. What are the chances now that you will get wiped out in the 1,000 flips? Turns out to be less than 5 percent because now we need to get a net of 100 losing coin flips in the 1,000 flips and the chances of that are very small.

One of the key factors to consider is that the return and risk are asymmetrical. How can that be when the odds are 50–50 on each coin flip? Shouldn't I always end up with roughly $100 at the end of the game? Nope!

Let's simplify the game for purposes of demonstration. Let's assume that you are going to bet $100 on each coin flip. Unfortunately, you lose the first flip. There. You've lost all your money. You don't get to play the game anymore.

Let's start over. This time you win the first flip so you have $200 in your account. But then you lose the next two flips. You're wiped out again and don't get to play the game.

Do you see a pattern developing? If you do well, you still have a chance of getting wiped out. But if you are wiped out, you never get another chance of doing well. That is why the game is asymmetrical. Each flip is 50–50 but getting wiped out means that you don't get to play the game anymore.

That is the situation we have with trading. You may have a good system, but getting wiped out means you don't get to trade anymore to take advantage of that good system. But making money in the beginning helps you from getting wiped out but doesn't completely eliminate the prospect. As a result, we need to have proper risk management to make sure that we can end up with enough of a chance to make money that the chance of getting wiped out and not getting to play the game is eliminated.

Risk management is really another name for asset allocation. How we allocate our precious resources is a major determinant of our eventual profit.

Risk management determines how fast or slow we grow our portfolio. Our portfolio will grow too slowly if we take too little risk, but we will have little chance of being wiped out. On the other hand, our portfolio may grow very quickly if we take big risks, but we run a high chance of getting wiped out. Can we find the point where we have little risk of being wiped out yet still have a great chance of growing profits in a dramatic fashion?

Keep reading to find out.

HOW TO MAKE SURE WE ARE NEVER WIPED OUT

There was a famous Greek philosopher named Zeno. He developed something that has come to be known as Zeno's Paradox. I like to use it as an example of how the methods that I'm going to show you ensure that you don't get wiped out.

Zeno presented the following situation: An archer shoots an arrow to a target. At some point, the arrow reaches a halfway point. Okay, from that halfway point to the target there is another halfway point. And from that new halfway point to the target is a farther halfway point. How can the arrow ever reach the target?

I can't answer that paradox but I do know that we can use a similar idea when designing a risk management scheme. We can make sure that our equity never gets wiped out.

GOOD RISK MANAGEMENT: FIXED FRACTIONAL

The core technique for risk management is called *fixed fractional* because we risk a fixed fraction of our portfolio on every trade. If you always risk a fixed percentage of your account, you will risk fewer dollars on each trade as you lose money.

For example, let's assume that you have $100,000 in your account and you decide to risk 1 percent on each trade. Assume that you lose the maximum on the first three trades. You will lose $1,000 on the first trade, which is 1 percent of $100,000. You now have $99,000 in your account. That means you can only risk $990 on the next trade. You are only allowed to risk 1 percent of the total equity in your account. You only have $99,000 in your account after the first trade so 1 percent of $99,000 is $990. You now lose on your second trade, leaving you with $98,010 in your account. It should now be no surprise that you will only risk $980 on your next trade.

Just like Zeno's Paradox, there appears to be an infinite number of times you can risk 1 percent. Of course, the real world is not so paradoxical. You will eventually run your account down to a level where you cannot put on any more trades. Nonetheless, the fact that every one of your losing trades is smaller means that you can withstand a lot of pain before you are effectively out of the game. This simple method can keep you in the game for months or years. Hopefully, that amount of time will allow you to get your trading act together and start to make some money.

HOW MANY CONTRACTS SHOULD I PUT ON?

Suppose you have $100,000 in your trading account and you are risking 1 percent on each trade. You see a great trend analysis trade developing. It turns out that you will have to risk $750 on the trade per contract. How many contracts should you put on?

Basically, you take the risk that you are allowed for that currency pair and divide the risk per contract into that risk. That gives you the number of contracts that you are allowed.

The rule is that you can only risk 1 percent of your $100,000 on each trade. That means that you can only put on one contract since you are allowed to risk $1,000 and each contract is a risk of $750. Thus, risking two contracts would be $1,500 and that would be too much risk for the portfolio. So you only do one contract.

Don't change the stop just because you want to do two contracts. You should always pick the optimal stop point and then see how many contracts you are allowed to buy, not the other way round!

The risk management rule is there to make sure you stick to the self-discipline necessary to make money in the markets and not get blown out by a few bad trades.

One of the potential problems with restricting your risk this way is that you need to have a large bankroll. It is hard to trade forex using standard contracts without risking at least $750 per contract. That means that you must have $75,000 in your account to stick to the 1 percent rule. Many traders do not have that much money in their accounts.

So you have two choices. First is to trade the mini- or even micro-contracts that are available from many brokers. This means that you will be risking $75 on a mini-contract rather than $750 on a standard contract. Note also that using a mini-contract allows you to take any intermediate amount of risk up to your risk limit. The second choice is to earn more money to deposit into your account.

HIGHLY CORRELATED POSITIONS

Based on the risk management rules, you cannot be trading highly correlated pairs as if they were separate positions. For example, EUR/USD, USD/CHF, and GBP/USD are highly correlated. You should apply the 1 percent criterion to all of your positions in all of these pairs all the time.

For example, you are risking $750 on a position in USD/CHF and you see an opportunity to enter a similar position in EUR/USD that would be a risk of $800. Nope. You are not allowed to do that trade because it is too highly correlated with the first position. You are more than doubling up the risk.

What this means is that you should pick the best opportunity in each group. You can't put on all the channel breakout trades in all currencies at the same time. You need to pick the best one of the bunch and pass on the rest of the trades.

My way of doing this is to put in all the orders and wait for one to be filled. I then cancel all the other similar orders. For example, I see a channel breakout trade coming up in EUR/USD, USD/CHF, and GBP/USD. I'll put in all three orders. Once I'm filled in one of them, I cancel the orders in the other two.

Basically, I'm saying that I take the strongest of the bunch and cancel the rest. My reasoning is that the first one to break out is likely the best trade of the three so that is the one I want to jump on.

KELLY FORMULA

Now I want to show you how to turbo-charge your returns. The fixed fractional method is an excellent tradeoff between risk and reward. It gives you a good return for the risk you take. It is not designed to take the least risk nor is it designed to maximize your profit.

The Kelly Formula, also called the Kelly Criterion, is a very different risk management method. It is designed to maximize profit but takes much larger risks than the fixed fractional method.

The Kelly Formula was originated by a Bell Labs scientist named John Kelly who was trying to maximize the amount of data that could go through a telecommunications pipe. His boss, Claude Shannon, realized that the formula could be used for gambling and he applied it to blackjack successfully. My friend Ed Thorpe, most famous for his book *Beat the Dealer* (Vintage, 1966), also successfully extended it to the stock market.

But Kelly is also playing with fire. It can also show some massive losses. It's hard for most traders to use. So let's look at the underlying concepts of Kelly. And let's assume that we are using profitable systems.

First, Kelly grows profits geometrically rather than arithmetically. An arithmetical growth in equity is a straight line. A geometric growth in equity is a curved live that accelerates through time.

A geometric curve also means that the returns on a portfolio of trades is not even. That means that the returns on wins are bigger than losses.

There is a concept called the *law of large numbers*. A Swiss mathematician, Jakob Bernoulli, developed this in a treatise published in 1713.

He proposed that the expectation of a particular series approaches the ideal the larger the numbers being used. Let me translate. Let's say that we have a method that wins 45 percent of the time and the average winner is 2.2 times the average loser. Those numbers will only be true in the long run. Perhaps we only make three trades. All of them could be winners or all could be losers. That is not even close to the expectation of winning 45 percent of the time. However, the law of large numbers says that trade this method 100,000 times and the number of winners will be very, very close to the ideal 45 percent.

Let's look at another concept: expected value. The expected value, or EV, of a trade is simply the percent chance of winning times the average size of a winning trade minus the percent chance of losing times the average size of a losing trade.

$$EV = (\%W * AvgWinner) - (\%L * AvgLoser)$$

Simple!

But here's the key concept: Virtually everybody looks at every trade equally. I put on a channel breakout trade in EUR/JPY and another trade in USD/CHF using trend analysis. I look at each of those trades as equal. I will risk exactly the same for each trade. Perhaps I will risk 0.5 percent on each of them.

But those two trades are not equal. Perhaps one technique is better than the other technique. Perhaps one of the markets is in a well-defined trend and the other is drifting sideways. It makes more sense to weight better trades with a larger position.

Another way of describing risk management is asset allocation. Where and how you allocate your assets determines the risk in your portfolio. You will always want to invest in the best investments with larger positions than in your worst prospective investments. Normally, these investments are done based on the trader's gut: "I like this trade a lot so I think I'll put on a double-size position." Unfortunately, this is not a particularly rational way to allocate your assets.

You should be allocating resources based on rational criteria. Do you trade a particular pair better than other pairs? Is one of your trading methods better than the other ones? The answer is always yes.

You should be keeping track of all your trades. That way you can sort them and generate statistics about your trading. You are going to want to know what percent of your trades are winners and what percent are losers. You will also want to know the average size of your winners and losers. And, finally, you will want to know the greatest loss and greatest win. With these statistics, we can now start to allocate our risk in a completely different way.

The Kelly Formula, instead, allocates risk based on those stats that we are collecting. Here is the formula for determining how much to bet:

$$F = (bp - q)/b$$

Where F is the percentage of the current bankroll to wager, b is the average winner divided by the average loser, p is the probability of winning, which is the number of winners divided by the total number of trades, and q is the probability of losing, which is simply $1 - p$.

In plain English, we first take the average size of a winning trade and divide it by the average size of a losing trade. This is the odds we receive when we win versus what we give up when we lose, on average. So let's say that we make 100 pips on average when we win and lose 50 pips when we lose. The ratio is 2:1 so we would put in 2 for the b in the formula. P is the percent of total trades that are winners and q is simply 1 minus p.

So the formula is actually very easy to use. But I've made it really simple. Just go to http://investmentmentoringinstitute.com/kelly.php and fill in the blanks. Press "Calculate It!" and the amount of your bankroll that you should invest is displayed in red. Check it out!

Now, either use the Web calculator or your physical calculator or take your shoes off so we can do some calculating.

In general, the longer-term position techniques like channel breakout and trend analysis have a winning percentage of about 45 percent but the average winning trade is about 2.3 times the size of the losing trade. Let's plug those numbers into the Kelly Formula.

The Formula comes back and tells us that we should risk 22 percent of our bankroll on each trade. Let me explore this outcome because it reveals some very interesting concepts.

Basically, the Kelly Formula is telling us that we should put on a position large enough that we would lose 22 percent of our portfolio if there was an average loss. This may seem like an extraordinary amount of risk. And it is. But Kelly is based on maximizing profit, not finding a balance between risk and reward or trying to get the most conservative position.

Note that each trade loss would be 22 percent of the remaining portfolio. So we are effectively stopped from getting wiped out but we could suffer greatly. For example, we have our $100,000 account. I used the example of losing the maximum of 1 percent when using fixed fractional, so a loss would drop the account down to $99,000. But an average loss on Kelly would drop the account down to $78,000. Do another losing trade and the Kelly account would drop to $60,840. And so on.

Notice that I said *maximum loss* when describing the fixed fractional but *average loss* when describing the Kelly. The basic way of using Kelly is based on average loss, not maximum loss. This means that you may actually lose much more if the maximum loss is hit.

The idea of using the average loss works just fine in the context of gambling because the maximum loss and the average loss are often the same. You bet $2 on a nag and lose and the average loss and the maximum loss are the same.

But trading is different. The average loss is usually less than half of the maximum loss. So we can't use Kelly as is. We need to modify it to take into account this significant difference. We might otherwise find ourselves in deep trouble. I would also suggest that it would be psychologically debilitating to take such large losses.

One of the keys to using Kelly is to realize that it is a way to rationally determine the relative value of differing trades. Suppose that Kelly says you should risk 22 percent on this particular pair using this particular technique and says you should risk 11 percent on a different pair using the same technique. This clearly means that you should risk twice as much on the first trade as the second trade.

Perhaps that means that you use Kelly to modify the fixed fractional. In this case, perhaps you take 2 percent risk on the first trade and 1 percent on the second.

I suggest that you do not use the pure Kelly but use what is called a *fractional Kelly*. The most powerful fractional Kelly is a half-Kelly, which is when you put on a position half of what is recommended by Kelly. By doing this, it reduces your risk by 50 percent but only reduces your reward by a few percent. Your risk-adjusted return actually goes up. Still, this may mean that you are risking over 10 percent on a given trade.

Another way to modify Kelly is to use maximum loss in the calculation instead of the average loss. In other words, take the Kelly percent but divide into the largest loss, not the average loss, and you will be much more conservative.

So how should you use Kelly? Here's what I do.

First, I keep very good records of all my trades. That way I can see what the performance is of every technique and currency pair. That record keeping is invaluable for me to continue to grow as a trader.

I don't make any decisions on risk management until I have at least 30 trades. In addition, I really would prefer that I have 30 trades in different types of markets. How well does this technique/pair work in trending markets or sideways markets? With 30 trades, I can start to make some rational decisions.

Second, I use the Kelly weightings to change my fixed fractional trade sizes. My basic size is to risk 0.5 percent on each technique/pair. But I then adjust that by how big a proportion of my portfolio that Kelly says I should use. I look at this from a relative point of view. So, if I am using three different techniques for a given pair and the Kelly rankings are 5 percent, 10 percent, and 20 percent, then I will risk 0.5 percent for the middle technique/pair, half that for the first one, and double that for the last one.

The final way that I use Kelly is to take a small percentage of my portfolio, say 10 percent, and use the half-Kelly or the Kelly using the maximum loss on just that portion of the portfolio. I find that I can easily double my money on that portion and don't have any psychological issues with the potential losses.

Kelly is truly turbo-charging your returns. Using Kelly is the best way to create the most amount of money in the shortest time. However, it is also the scariest. I had a client who lost 97 percent of his portfolio in just six weeks using Kelly. But he ended up doubling his money in just another eight weeks. That shows the incredible power of Kelly, both good and bad.

TRADE YOUR EQUITY CURVE

You should also be thinking about the total risk in your portfolio. For example, while limiting the risk on any one position to 1 percent of the total account value, limit the risk on the whole portfolio to less than 5 percent, or perhaps even 3 percent. If every position were wiped out, you would be out 5 percent of your total account value. Big deal. You could survive that.

The idea is that you need to make sure that if a catastrophe like 9/11 occurs you will be able to survive it if every one of your positions were stopped out on one day.

I trade stocks and futures as well as forex. A lot of people have asked me exactly what I trade. I tell that I trade my equity curve. All that matters is that my equity is growing. The equity curve is simply a chart of the total equity in your account plotted once a day.

I know that I am doing correct trading actions if my equity chart starts in the lower left corner and is going to the upper right. That shows that my equity is growing. Well, theoretically, a growing equity curve could also mean that conditions are ripe for my methods of trading.

So what if my equity curve is declining? That means that either you are not executing flawlessly or that market conditions are not ripe for your method. In either case, you should be more cautious.

I suggest actually drawing a chart of your equity on a daily basis and then applying some technical method such as trend analysis to the chart. Take smaller positions or even stand aside if you see a downside breakout in your equity curve.

Then keep trading the methods on paper but not in the real world until your equity, on paper, has broken to a new high. This ensures that your methods are in tune with the market again and that you are executing flawlessly.

This method will ensure that you never have significant losses because you will be standing aside or trading smaller if you start on a losing streak.

TAKE A TIME OUT

Another key risk management rule is to take time off if you go through a losing streak. For example, perhaps you hit the 5 percent risk limit mentioned earlier. Take a break from trading. Clear your head. Go walk around the block.

People are tremendously attracted to doing stupid things after they have lost a good chunk of money. You won't have any objectivity. You won't be calm, cool, and collected.

In any case, it is better to take a couple of days off and come back to the markets with your head screwed on straight. Your mental state is the most influential factor in creating investment profits. Do not take it lightly.

Here's another related rule. Make sure that you do not lose more than 10 percent in one month. If you do, simply shut down trading and take a longer vacation. You need to make sure that you do not have a catastrophic month. This rule ensures that you will never have a disaster even if you are bleeding somewhat. Let me suggest that you shut down trading for a day whenever you suffer a 2 percent loss in one day. Take a day off. Take a week off if you suffer a 5 percent loss, and shut down for the month if you hit 10 percent.

I've used this rule when I've run professional trading desks and it works. I see a trader losing money and I probably see a trader that is probably suffering psychologically and won't be a good trader. I would send them off the desk to at least walk around the block. I have even sent them home for a week. We called it being put in the penalty box.

Now, some people would think that would be great. You lose money and get a paid vacation. But it's not that way with traders. They don't work for the salary but for the bonus. Taking time off reduces their ability to make more money trading and therefore their bonus. It's a punishment.

TURNING POOR SYSTEMS INTO GOOD SYSTEMS

Here's an interesting idea that I've never seen elsewhere. We can use good risk management to improve the profitability of trading methods. Let me show you how.

Although there are many reasons why trading systems look bad during testing, one common problem is that a system has shown a few huge losses during the testing period. Here is how risk management concepts can help.

Make a histogram of all the losses, making the left axis the size of the loss and the bottom axis the number of times that the loss occurred. What you will find is that most of the losses are moderate but there are several whopping losses. Simply look at the histogram to see where you could put a money management stop that would cut out most of the major losers but only account for a few trades.

For example, assume that you have 100 losses in your test. Ninety-five of the losses are $1,000, which you can financially (and psychologically) handle. However, there are five that are greater than $1,000, including a couple that are greater than $5,000. Change the rules for exiting positions to either the signal of the trading system or $1,000, whichever shows the least loss. You will find that you will reduce the total losses typically by 20 percent to 40 percent.

Once in a blue moon, a trade will show a big open loss only to turn around and move to a profit position. However, that outcome is so rare that this simple technique can turn many losing systems into profitable systems. In addition, it may significantly enhance nearly all systems.

HOW BIG A POSITION SHOULD I TAKE?

Here's what I recommend for weighting on each position. Why not start with 0.5 percent for each method/pair? In other words, let's say that you are trading trend analysis, channel breakout, and the Conqueror. You would risk a maximum total of 1.5 percent for each pair. That means that you will risk 0.5 percent for each method. Note that you could, at any given time, be risking zero, 0.5 percent, 1.0 percent, or 1.5 percent. Note that you will get to the maximum risk in only a few rare circumstances. I'll come back to this in a minute.

I recommend 0.5 percent in each position not because it is the best amount of risk to take but because it is a good starting point for traders. This amount is usually a small amount to lose for anyone.

A beginning trader should likely start with 0.25 percent for each technique/instrument pair. That means that using four techniques on one given pair will mean that the total risk could get as high as 1.0 percent (though this is highly unlikely).

Then, start to increase the amount of risk as you feel more confident about the techniques. Go to 0.3 percent, then 0.4 percent, and so on up to the point that you feel comfortable. You probably don't want to get to a point where you have a total risk of over 5 percent in any given pair. But the point is to develop the confidence to increase risk as you develop as a trader.

Use the concept of changing the size from Kelly and apply to the fixed fractional.

THE BOTTOM LINE: DIVERSIFY THROUGH TIME

What is the bad news of using strict risk management? Not much.

First, you have to be much more disciplined in your trading. You have to do a little more work to figure out your risk on each position and the total portfolio risk. Frankly, this is no big task.

Second, your return may go down, though this is not a given. For most people, their returns will skyrocket. Generally, traders with powerful risk management rules will not have years that put them in the top 10 percent every year. It is difficult to have 100 percent years using these rules. It takes a lot of risk to make a ton of money.

However, the risk-adjusted return (the return in a portfolio divided by the standard deviation of the monthly returns) will shoot higher. You will be producing lower returns but with sharply reduced risk.

In addition, although you will not be number one in any given year, you will be number one for any given five years. It was largely using this technique that got me a top ranking for my Macro hedge fund and for my stock-picking letter. I was never top ranked for any given year but always ended up in the top 25 percent. After a few years of being in the top 25 percent, I ended up at or near the number one ranking. It was this pattern of consistently high returns that did the trick.

This chapter has put you in a very elite group. You now know more about risk management than probably 95 percent of investors. You now know how to control risk at a level only the most sophisticated hedge funds do. This is a huge advantage in the fight for forex profits.

Let me prove this. Most institutional investors are not allowed to have less than 97 percent of their money under management to be in cash. They certainly aren't allowed to be short. This applies to mutual funds, segregated funds, and union funds. The manager would be fired if they were to go 50 percent into cash! The basic concept is that the investor wants to invest in, say, natural resources, and then they buy a natural resources mutual fund. The manager is supposed to stay fully invested in natural resources stocks and not deviate from that mandate. So they have to stay fully invested in natural resource stocks even in the midst of the bear market.

Now, grab the next 100 retail investors on the street and ask them if they use any risk management. The answer from only a few will be that they use some protective stop orders. The rest will think you are nuts.

That leaves only some hedge funds that use proper money management. Welcome to the risk management elite!

Sharply controlling the risk in your portfolio can keep you in the game and even beat the game. Use the fixed fractional or Kelly method to calculate how large your position should be, use some type of portfolio risk management to control the total risk in your portfolio, and make sure that you have the right attitude to keep trading. If you follow these rules, you will find a sharp increase in both your profits and your confidence.

CHAPTER 8

Slingshot

One of the keys to making money in forex is the ability to filter out bad trades. I've shown you the ADX filter in Chapter 2, which can eliminate a lot of bad trades but only a few good trades. I've shown you the Bishop and rejection rule in Chapters 2 and 3, which allow you to get out of trades with small losses before they turn into big losses or take profits as the trend changes.

The slingshot is an interesting extension of the basic concepts behind trend analysis. However, the extensions demonstrate some key concepts that can significantly enhance profitability and reduce risk.

The slingshot uses these critical concepts to create a method that contains some different ways of looking at the market. For example, I will show you a unique method of creating profits in the market, maximum excursion analysis (MEA). The basic concept behind this analysis came from Kent Calhoun but I have taken his ideas and made a general principle behind them. This is a method never revealed since Kent stopped providing information to the market. I don't use the same method as Kent but show you an adaptive way of achieving the same thing.

I will also use the slingshot to show you the importance of using confirmations as a method of reducing risk.

THE IMPORTANCE OF MINIMIZING LOSSES

Reducing the number of bad trades can dramatically enhance the profitability of a method even though we have strictly limited the size of the potential losses. A typical trend following system, which I prefer, will only make money on about 45 percent of trades but the winning trades will be about 2.5 times the size of the average loss. Let's assume, for simplicity sake, that each loser is $1 and each winner is $2.50. That means that you should have a profit of $57 (45 times $2.50 minus 55 times $1.00) after 100 trades.

Reducing the number of losing trades by 10, or about 20 percent, improves the profitability dramatically. The percent of the 100 trades that are now winners increases to 55 and the number of losing trades drops to 45. Now the profit is $92.50 (55 times $2.50 minus 45 times $1.00). That is a dramatic increase in profit of 62 percent! A small change in the ratio of winners to losers can create a dramatic change in the profitability of a method. This suggests that we must be always searching for ways to decrease the number of losers compared to the number of winners in order to boost profitability.

Note that the rejection rule and last bar method increase the number of losing trades significantly but the total dollars lost declines. We have substituted a larger number of small losses instead of a fewer number of large losses (or kept the size of the losers constant but dramatically boosted the size of our winners). These changes sharply enhance our profits.

It is profitable for you to keep track of these kinds of statistics for your own trading. Then you can concentrate on fixing that part of the equation that you really need to work on. Is it cutting losses? Increasing the size of your winners?

I mainly focus on eliminating losses or minimizing the size of losses. The reason is that this enhances my psychological ability to trade. I'll talk more about that in a later chapter but let me mention a few things here.

One of the most difficult things for traders to do is to suffer through a string of losses. Most people will stop trading a method if they have three losing trades in a row. They will say that the system is flawed or they are flawed and stop trading. So it is particularly important to attack the inevitable losses that come with trading. Reducing losses in a method by several a year could mean the difference between my psychologically continuing to trade, or stopping.

Psychologically, a small or miniscule loss may be the same as no loss so it is also important for me to strive to reduce the size of losses. My goal is always to reduce the size of my losses to a level that I won't remember tomorrow if I had a loss today. I am not likely to have any psychological bad effects from a trade that I can't remember!

BEWARE OF TAKING PROFITS TOO EARLY

"You can't go broke taking a profit" is something I've heard many times over the last 30 years. But what I've found is that you *can* go broke taking a profit.

Every method has a certain number of losses and a certain number of gains. That is the nature of every method. There can be variances around that number for short periods of time but not over the long run. Let's go back to our example of losing $1.00 on each losing trade and making $2.50 on each winning trade and 45 percent of our trades are winners.

We know through simple math that this is a winning method. But what if we took profits every time we had a $1.00 profit? That would make this a money-losing method immediately. We are losing on more trades than we are winning so making/losing equal amounts of money on each trade is a surefire way to lose money.

Realistically, though, taking quick profits will likely boost the number of winning trades to losing trades. This may be enough to make this a profitable system. However, we would have to boost the number of winning trades compared to the losing trades by a large amount to equal the profits of the original ratio.

All methods have losing trades. That is the price of playing the game. We need a certain number of winning trades of a certain size to pay for those losses. The winning trades that are beyond that level create the profit for us.

Every method has a natural profile of winning and losing trades, their size and frequency. Let's assume that you are using a winning method. Cutting the size of the winners will usually cause a higher number of winners but at a much smaller size. I may cut the size of the winner from $2.50 to $1.00. The average size of my winner is now just 40 percent of the previous size. That means that I must have 150 percent more winners than I did before to equal the dollars that I had made before in my trading. Remember that I was making only 45 percent of my trades as profits with the remainder being losses. Adding 150 percent of the 45 percent winners would mean that I would have to have more winners than I have trades to equal the profits of the original method. That's impossible.

Basically, the base method lost on slightly more than 50 percent of the trades but the winning trades were 2.5 times the size of the losing trades. It is impossible to make as much money as this method if I cut the profits to only 1 times the size of the losing trades because I would have to have more winning trades than I have trades to make that much money.

It comes back to the old trading adage of letting your profits run and cutting your losses.

We need to be careful when we take profits too early. Most of the techniques in this book are trend-following techniques. That means that we want to follow the trend as long as it is trending. Generally, we have no idea of how far a trend will go. So we want to give that method as much room as possible to let the trend make us as much money as possible.

Basically, we let the trend run until we are stopped out. I have said that protective stops should have two attributes. First, they should filter out random noise. We don't want to be stopped out because of some blip in the market, only because something significant has happened. Second, we only want to be stopped out when we are wrong.

In the case of a trend-following technique, we only want to be stopped out when the trend is no longer our friend and the market has turned neutral or bearish. So why would we ever want to take profits before getting stopped out? There are two reasons: psychological profits and confirmations. We'll explore both in the pages that follow.

PSYCHOLOGICAL PROFITS

Most beginning traders are stunned when I tell them that most of my trades are losers. They think that it is impossible to make money when most of your trades are losers. They think that a master trader should win most, maybe nearly all, of their trades. In fact, I doubt if any of the top ten traders in the world win on most of their trades.

Trading profits generally follow the 80/20 Principle, or the Pareto Principle. It states that 80 percent of your profits will come from 20 percent of your trades. While this may not *literally* be true, the theory holds. Most of your profits will come from a small minority of your trades.

This can be psychologically difficult. You may go months without really seeing a big-profit trade. We are only trading five major pairs so we do not have the luxury of a diversified portfolio. That means that we can easily go months of little winners and little losers.

Naturally, there will come a time when we see several or more losing trades in a row. If you follow my directions in this book then none of these will be big losers. Each one will be trivial. But the cumulative effect of this string of paper cuts will begin to wear on your emotions. You may become frustrated or bored with the action or lack of action. You may begin to doubt the value of the method, or worse, the value of yourself as a trader.

Both concepts will lead to further losses as you break your discipline. Perhaps you will stop trading altogether.

The point is that a series of losing trades, even small losers, or a losing streak can break you psychologically. Chapter 9 will cover this in more detail, but it is important to bring it up here.

One solution to psychological stress is to boost the number of winning trades. The potential for losing streaks decreases and the positive reinforcement that comes from having a winning streak increases. Even having the occasional small winner can create a much more positive emotional and psychological state of mind and thus enhance the profitability of the trader through greater discipline.

Adding a smattering of winning trades can create a better mind-set to make money. It will give the positive feedback that will help to create the discipline to be consistent and persistent in the face of a losing streak. Why? Because the losing streak will be reduced or limited by the addition of some small winning trades.

CONFIRMATIONS

A *confirmation* comes when a signal occurs and there is another indicator that agrees with the signal. The average directional index (ADX) Filter is an example of a confirmation. The ADX must be climbing to confirm the breakout signal of, say, channel breakout. In effect, there must be two signals before a trade is placed.

Confirmations are an important concept because you are effectively making sure that the original signal is correct before taking action. This reduces losing trades but at the cost of occasionally missing out on a winning trade. Generally speaking, this is a good tradeoff and net profits will increase. In addition, you will trade less. This may be a good or a bad thing depending on your psychology or situation. Will you get bored due to less trading and have your discipline break down or will the reduction in trading losses increase your discipline?

I was working at a major bank running a trading desk. For the life of me, I could not see any good trades. This drifted on for a couple of weeks. Finally, my boss, the treasurer, came over to me and asked me why I wasn't trading. I told him that I couldn't see any good trades. He thundered that I was paid to trade. I was dumbfounded and retorted that I thought I was paid to make money. As you can imagine, I lost the argument so I was sentenced to trading trades I didn't like in as small a size as possible so I would lose as little as possible.

MAXIMUM EXCURSION ANALYSIS

I first ran across the idea of maximum excursion analysis (MEA) from Kent Calhoun. He didn't call it that but I took the idea from him and made it more general than what he was doing. He basically looked at different types of technical signals in futures, such as head and shoulders or breakouts, and measured how much did the futures contract go after that signal.

For example, how far did the market move after breaking the 55-day high? (It is actually more difficult to answer this question than it sounds. What objective criteria will you use to determine the farthest that the price went? Oh, it went up 500 pips. But what about the 5,000 pips it went up over the next year? Do you count that as part of this signal or is that just drift in the price?) However you determine this, it will form a classic bell curve.

One of the problems in Kent's method is that he plotted the absolute price changes that came from a signal. That meant that a signal when EUR/USD is 1.5000 was treated the same as when it was 0.8000. Clearly, the moves will be bigger when the price is higher than when it is lower. However, the percentage move will likely be about the same. So we need to adjust the maximum excursion to the price level. This can be done by simply tracking the maximum excursions as percents rather than as absolute price movements.

So now you have adjusted everything to percentages. You will now have a nice bell curve that shows how much the price moves after breaking a key technical pattern. Let's assume for a moment that it shows that, given current market levels, it will gain 100 pips 90 percent of the time, 200 pips 62 percent of the time, and 300 pips 32 percent of the time.

We could put in an order to take profits of 100 pips and we would gain that profit about 90 percent of the time. We would take a profit of 200 pips about 62 percent of the time if we put in a limit order to take profits at that level and so on.

Note that 10 percent of the time, in our example, the price doesn't even go 100 pips after breaking this key technical level. Also remember that this example is only an example, and is only for purposes of explanation.

We now know what the chances are of what amount of money that we are going to make on a trade. We now can construct a strategy to take that into account. For example, I now know that 90 percent of the time I can make 100 pips when this particular technique is triggered. That means that only 10 percent of the time do I run the risk of losing money and even part or most of that 90 percent will actually be going past the 100 pips level and going to a new level. Now I can put in an entry stop when the technical trigger occurs and a limit order at the same time to take profits when the market moves 100 pips.

There is another amazing idea that comes from MEA: You can turn losing techniques into winners.

There are a million trading techniques out there. Most of them are garbage. They are consistent losers. But the principle of MEA can turn them into winners.

Typically, a trading method has an entry and an exit rule. They are usually the same rule. For example, a moving average crossover method will buy when the shorter moving average crosses above the longer moving average and then reverse and go short when the shorter moving average crosses below the longer moving average. This can be a profitable method if the length of the moving averages are correct but can also be a losing technique if the length is wrong.

I know that the 5/10 moving average crossover is a money-losing system. (Go long when the five-day moving average crosses above the 10-day moving average and go short when the five-day moving average crosses below the 10-day moving average.) You should never use this system. But what if we apply MEA to it?

Now we can do the study and see if you can make money looking for small profits when the shorter moving average crosses the longer moving average. In fact, you can turn this losing system into a profitable system. (I'm not giving you the exact parameters for making a profit because I don't want anyone to actually go out and do this. It's still not particularly profitable.) This is astounding because we have turned an unprofitable trading method into a profitable method.

I've not seen anyone really do any research into the use of MEA as a means of creating and/or enhancing profits of trading techniques. In fact, remember the multiunit tactic for the inside days technique (Chapter 6) where we took a quick 20-pip profit? That was an example of MEA.

USING THE SLINGSHOT FOR PROFITS

I went through this preamble because I wanted to give some of the flavor behind the concept of the slingshot. It was designed to not trade unless there are multiple confirmations that the coast is clear to trade.

Every technique in this book is complementary with the other techniques. They may all be profitable by themselves but are far more profitable when combined. For example, the main purpose of the channel breakout is to ensure that we catch the big move.

One of the purposes of the slingshot is to take profits on strength. It is there to boost the number of winners in relation to the number of losers. In addition, it shows the concept of confirmation and how it can be used in a trading method. It is similar to trend analysis in that we are always looking for similar swing highs and lows and looking for breakouts using those highs and lows. But it differs from trend analysis in that it is looking for confirmations and also takes profits.

Let's start to look at the rules. In Figure 8.1, the first data point is to identify what I have labeled Key High. The key high is any high that is higher than the previous high. So in this case the key high is the first swing high since early December.

We then identify a Key Low. It is also a swing low. This key low must be at least a two-bar swing low. My preference is a three-bar low but I'll take a two-bar low.

The Slingshot High is the critical high in the technique. Let's examine it a little closer. Note that this slingshot high is a failure. This had been a strong bull market to this point but this bar failed to make new high. The slingshot high doesn't have to be a failure, but it helps.

There are two confirmations for the slingshot high. The first is that the slingshot high must be at least three bars from a previous higher bar. In this case, the previous bar with a higher high is actually the key high. It won't usually be the key high, but it was in this case. The second is that the previous high bar must not be more than 20 days from the slingshot high. Once again, the previous high bar is the key high bar and it is six days from the slingshot high.

These two confirmations sharply reduce the risk in the trade by ensuring that you are only getting into the trade with the odds in your favor. The first confirmation makes sure that you are not in a running market and that the market is creating a solid formation. In effect, it is ensuring that you are not buying the top of a formation but the beginning of a new trend. The second confirmation makes sure that you are not trying to pick the bottom in a market. Note that these two confirmations make sure that you are not trying to get in on the key high but only after certain price action has shown that the bull leg is over.

I haven't put it on the chart but we are also going to use the ADX Filter on this method (see Chapter 2 for more on ADX).

We now look to sell on a break of the key low. This confirms that the trend is now down and we can get short. Your first protective stop loss is the slingshot high. In fact, I like to make this a reversal stop so that we not only exit our short position but go long. Remember, a failed signal is a signal!

Unlike trend analysis, which is designed to try to stay in the position for as long as possible, we are going to enter a profit-taking limit order.

The first profit objective is calculated this way. Take the difference between the slingshot high and the key low. Now subtract that value from

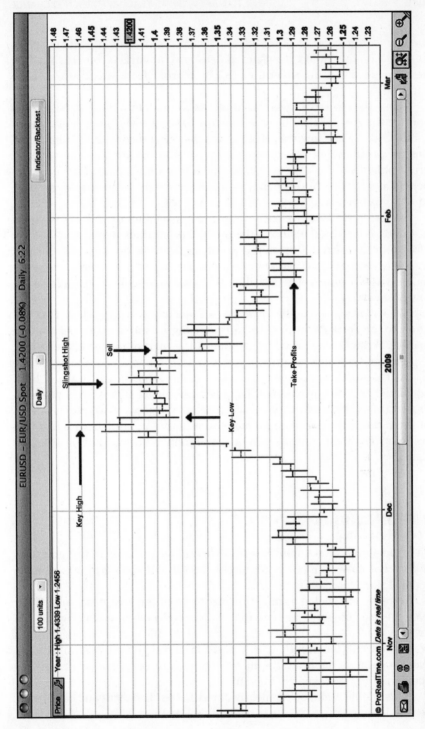

FIGURE 8.1 A Slingshot Trade

the key low. You will take profits at that point on half of your position. Yes, you really should be using at least two contracts on this method because we are using several methods to profit from this method. Let's carry on.

Raise the stop to a level that protects 25 percent of your profits when you hit the first profit objective. In this case, the slingshot high was at 1.4363 and the key low was at 1.3826 so the difference was 537 pips. I call this the profit target. We subtract 537 pips from the key low and we get a profit objective of 1.3289, which we hit where I have placed an arrow labeled Take Profits. At this point, we would move the protective stop down to 134 pips below the key low of 1.3826 or 1.3692.

We are now going to use a trailing stop based on the factors we have just outlined. Move the stop to the original profit objective of 1.3289 if the price moves down 1.5 times the profit target from the key low. Keep it trailing after that by 50 percent of a profit target. In this example, the profit target was 537 pips so use a trailing stop that is roughly 268 pips from the low of the move.

We will also use the Bishop as an exit technique for slingshot. That will often be the normal exit plan should we really get into a major bear or bull market. We will also be taking profits as the market moves lower. But it depends on how many contracts you have.

At the point where we have reached the profit target, we will have liquidated half of our position. Liquidate another half if we reach a level of two times the profit target. Liquidate another half if we reach a level of three times the profit target and so on until you are left with just one contract. The final contract will be exited only on a stop out or a Bishop signal.

THE MINI-SLINGSHOT

The mini-slingshot is a shorter-term swing trader variation of the slingshot. It does not have as much confirmation and it is designed to take a quick profit. Take a look at Figure 8.2.

Here we are seeing a similar formation from the previous figure. However, we are going to eliminate the 20-day confirmation and leave just the two-day confirmation. We are also going to take 100 percent of the position off when we hit the profit target. We will raise our protective stop to break even as soon as the price has moved 50 percent of the way from the Go Long point to the Take Profits point.

This simple technique is clearly closer to trend analysis and can almost be considered a profit-taking version of that method.

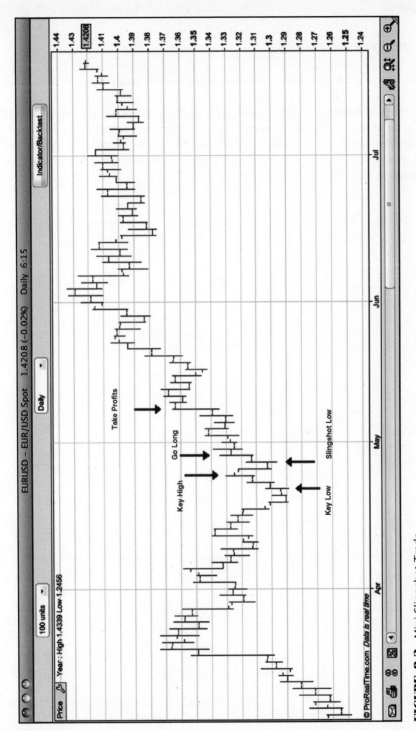

FIGURE 8.2 Mini-Slingshot Trade

THE BOTTOM LINE

The slingshot has a particular spot in our toolbox of trading techniques. It is there to provide us with a low-risk trading method that will take a higher number than normal profitable trades. It will not make us as much money at the end of the year as other techniques, such as channel break-outs, but it will be profitable and it will create a positive psychological environment to help us have the right mind-set to make money in all the other methods.

CHAPTER 9

The Psychology of Successful Trading

I t is a well-known fact that roughly 90 percent of forex traders lose money, about 5 percent break even, and 5 percent make money. Why? And what can be done about it?

The answers to these questions may be the most critical for any forex traders. This chapter explores these issues and attempts to highlight ways that traders can become profitable in their forex trading. The psychology of trading is the most important factor for determining the success of your trading.

There are numerous trading systems on the market that are profitable. There are numerous trading advisors and newsletters that have had long-profitable track records. Yet the average speculator is a losing trader. The average speculator, when handed sound advice, will still lose money.

I have been writing on this subject since my book *Commodity Spreads* (John Wiley & Sons) was published in 1982. I feel that understanding the psychology of trading is vitally important for myself as a professional trader and for you, the intelligent reader of this book.

I have given lectures on this subject mainly to futures and forex traders though the years. The first thing that I do is ask how many people in the audience have made significant money over the prior two years. I have had only one person raise their hand in the hundreds of people who have attended the lecture. I then ask how many had made significant money over the prior year. I get a few hands. The point: The vast majority of traders don't make money.

I have often wondered why. After all, the vast majority of the people at the lectures are successful people in their businesses. It costs about $500 to attend the conference, and the attendees may also be paying for travel and hotels to attend the conference. It takes a certain amount of money to spend a minimum of $500 to gain some insight into trading.

There are few people who attend these conferences that are not very successful people. Why is it that they can be successful doctors, lawyers, and business owners yet cannot trade forex? What is it about forex trading that is so hard?

WHY DO YOU TRADE?

I ask the audience members why they trade. Of course, the answer is to make money. I ask them if they are really sure. By this time, they are starting to second-guess their first answer. But, in the final analysis, they stick with their answer: that they are trading so that they can make money. I think that that is completely wrong. I think that people trade for tons of other reasons and that making money is a relatively minor reason. Nobody really knows why each individual person trades but there are many reasons other than making money.

I first discovered this about 20 years ago. Back in the 1970s, I managed futures money with a partner. We offered two different accounts to our prospective clients. The first account traded only commodity spreads and was making 200 percent per year while the second account traded only outright positions and was making about 100 percent per year (please note that these returns were so high because I didn't know as much as I do now about risk and money management and we were simply taking far too much risk).

Of course, everybody opened up a spread account because it was making 200 percent per year. Within six months, nearly everybody had shifted their account to the outright program in spite of the fact that it returned only half as much! This stunned us because we always assumed that people invested in futures to make money. In fact, they were involved, I believe, for the action. They would call us up when they were invested in the spread account and ask how their account was doing. We would respond that they made $12.50 the previous day because a back spread in the corn market has moved one-quarter of a cent. On the other hand, they would call about their outright account and we could say that the value of the account had moved $1,000 because of some big move in the bellies.

The point is that they wanted the action of the futures markets, not the profits. Their primary motivation was action and making money was secondary. It's okay to pay to see a movie because of the entertainment value. To these traders, losing money trading was the price of admission to a fun and exciting game.

This was my first clue that making money is secondary to other considerations with many people.

I believe that there are many other reasons why people trade. In the example just given, the clients were more interested in the excitement of trading than in the making of money. They wanted to feel that jolt of adrenaline that comes from trading. They liked the high of having the account value go up and perhaps even liked the adrenaline hit when the account value went down.

In the lecture, I ask attendees how they feel when they have bought a market and it is moving strongly higher. People in the audience said that they felt great; they felt high! And they said that they felt terrible when they were losing money.

It is common for people to equate the forex market to Las Vegas. People know that they will lose money when they go to Las Vegas and yet they still go because of the excitement and entertainment they receive. Except for card-counters in blackjack, nobody goes to Las Vegas to make money. Nobody plays roulette with the idea that they will make a lot of money or will be able to make a living doing it. They do it for the action.

Many people trade forex to provide a diversion from their regular life, perhaps because they feel that it is boring or not stimulating enough. They could call their bookie or they could call their broker. It beats sitting at home and watching TV.

Another reason that many people like to invest in forex is because they like to solve the puzzle of what makes the market go up and down. They want to be able to predict the market.

It's interesting to note that nearly all the articles and books written about forex trading are about entry and exit techniques. Yet trading techniques developed by Richard Donchian in the 1960s have been shown to make money for every year since then. We already know techniques that make money, yet 90 percent of traders lose money. Odd? Yes! It is clear to me that it is more important for many people to continue to figure out what makes the market tick or to figure out new entry and exit techniques than to make money. Rather than use the old tried-and-true techniques and make money, they prefer to try to figure out new techniques.

There is a common desire in many to want to figure out puzzles. The market is a very challenging puzzle to be solved and attracts many people to do just exactly this. They are fascinated by the puzzle. They want to find a new way to beat the market.

Many traders believe that there is an underlying truth to the market or perhaps a powerful underlying pattern or force. They, therefore, believe that they should spend a tremendous amount of time trying to understand that underlying force. For example, many people spend countless hours and days trying to understand Gann or Elliott on the assumption that if they can just crack the code they will become rich beyond their wildest dreams. Or that if they just study harder they will understand the teachings of the guru that they are subscribing to.

These traders focus on trying to unlock the secrets of the universe as the way of making money rather than go directly to the subject of making money. They end up spending a tremendous amount of time on the study of esoteric theory and not on trading the markets. When they do trade the markets, they often stop trading after just a few losing trades because they assume that they do not understand the secrets of the universe well enough and should go back to studying.

Take a look at the popularity of the literature and lectures about trading systems. The basic concept behind trading systems is that there is a mathematical model that will create profits. I agree that this is true. The continuing success of Donchian's basic systems, mentioned earlier, shows that trading systems can make money. However, many people like to invent their own systems or modify other systems that they have bought or read about. One problem with this is that they spend all their time trying to perfect the system rather than make money. They often become obsessed with fine-tuning their system rather than simply using an imperfect system. Of course, no system is perfect so they end up spending all their free time on the system instead of making money. The chase of the system is more important than making money. The perfection of the system becomes much more important than the point of the system, which is supposedly to make money.

A number of years ago, I had the opportunity to train traders from Korea. I had six months to turn them into profit-making traders. They each had $100,000 to trade. I had three groups of six traders for each six-month period.

I decided to give the initial six trader-trainees a liberal arts education about trading. I taught them everything about trading under the sun. I even had guest lecturers teach them about subjects that I was not an expert in, like Elliott Wave.

One of the guest lecturers was a good friend of mine who was an Elliott Wave fanatic and had been trading using Elliott Wave for about eight years. I left him with the students while he gave the lecture. At the end of the lecture, I came back in and started to ask him some questions about his trading that I thought would be informative to my students.

I asked him point-blank, "Why do you use Elliott Wave?"

He said, "There is no greater feeling in the world than to have analyzed the wave structure of a move and to buy right at the absolute bottom of Wave Two!"

He then jerked his thumb at me and said to the students, "It's so much better than trading the boring way that Courtney does!"

I use many of those tried-and-true trend-following techniques and my techniques never allow me to buy the bottom of any move.

The point of this is that my guest lecturer was far more interested in being right than in making money.

This is one of the critical concepts necessary to become a profitable trader. You must focus on making money, not on being right. In fact, super-analyst Ned Davis once wrote a slim book called *Being Right or Making Money*. Notice that it's not called *Being Right and Making Money*. To both of us, trying to be right is a block to making money.

Trying to be right means that your ego is wrapped up in the outcome of the trade. You will, therefore, have the tendency to want to hold onto losers longer than you should. They will become larger than they should be for you to have trading success. You will not have cut your losses short. In addition, you will take off winning trades quickly with only small gains because taking a profit will vindicate you and show that you are right.

A slight twist on this is that many traders feel the need to validate themselves as people. Having a winning trade is a way to validate themselves and make them feel good about themselves. It shows them that they are smart and clever because they were able to peg the market.

I once did a session with a new mentoring student of mine. I spent the first three sessions dealing only with the psychology of trading. His background is in the mental health profession so he was very self-aware. Here is his list of what motivates him to trade:

You need to be smart to do this so being successful will validate that I am a smart person. I don't have anywhere else to go (quoting the movie An Officer and a Gentleman*). There are no jobs in my small rural Florida town. Have my wife feel secure and proud of me is the number one motivator for me to be a trader. Need to feel that I can be part of the financial world because I have just failed as a stock broker. I should be able to do this. I would be sexier if I was a good trader. I like the idea of the freedom and not chained to someone else's authority. I'd love to have a skill to teach to one of my nephews. I'm not the kind of guy who mows lawns. I'd like to have lifestyle freedom like travel whenever I want. I want my mother and stepfather to be proud of me. My stepfather made a lot of money trading futures in '70s and '80s then lost most of it in '90s. I want to be better than his stepfather. I am competing with my stepfather for my mother's attention. I am also competing with my brothers.*

Whew!

Trying to be right also creates a tendency to cause overanalysis of a position. Some traders will overanalyze a position to make sure that they are right and then end up missing the move. They were never wrong, but they didn't make any money.

There are also many people who trade forex because of the image that it projects. Forex traders are sometimes thought of as rogues. You can project an image of sophistication if you trade foreign exchange.

There are people who like to discuss their speculative adventures to their friends and associates or at parties as an image enhancement tool. They want to show off their knowledge or project an image to others. It can sound much more impressive to other people if you are sitting around talking about your last trade in the euro market than what you normally do for a living.

A final common reason for trading forex is pure greed. But I am differentiating between trying to make money and the greed that is trying to make a big score quickly. You go to your job every day to make money, but you buy lottery tickets to make the big score.

Similarly, trading forex to make money is different than trying to make scads of money quickly. It is this type of greed that fuels the hype on the Internet and attracts people to those commercials on the radio and TV that suggest that you can make a huge percent profit in just 10 minutes every day. It is this greed that fuels the ads in other forex publications that show pictures of guys on the beach with their cell phone and a piña colada trading forex or posing in front of their Rolls Royce.

There are few endeavors in which you can make millions with just a small investment and trading forex is one of them. There is no question that the dream can come true in forex but, realistically, it never will. And the ways to achieve it being touted by forex promoters are certainly not the way to achieve it. Still, there are many new forex traders who trade forex to make a big score quickly.

I suggest that you take a few minutes to ponder why you are trading. There are no bad answers but it is important that one of the reasons is that you want to make money. All other reasons are okay. It is important to understand what makes you tick so that you can design your trading life to take it into account.

THE PRESSURES OF TRADING

The pressures of trading are extreme. You feel elation when you have a big winner and depression when you have a big loser. Unfortunately, these emotions are the enemy. You've got to overcome them. Many of the most successful traders that I have known have ice water running in their veins. They remain cool and calm no matter what good or bad events are swirling around them.

Legendary trader Richard Dennis stated that trading is almost against human nature. We have met the enemy and he is us.

Much of the issue of self-discipline is finding ways to overcome our natural impulses driven by fear and greed and the other motivations outlined in the beginning of this chapter. Perhaps we need to distract ourselves from what is really driving us to something more manageable that we can control.

The pressure of making and losing money creates a lack of objectivity that clouds your mind and therefore creates dubious trading ideas. The first goal is to reduce these pressures and help us become calm about our trading.

WHY DO YOU LOSE?

In my lectures, I ask the audience members to tell me why they lose money trading forex. I am always fascinated that they know exactly why they lose. Let me repeat. They know *exactly* why they lose.

I suggest you stop reading right now and write up a list of reasons why you lose. Go on, stop reading and start listing!

Back to the lecture. The traders quickly jump up and list off the reasons why they lose while I write them down. Let me show you the list from the last lecture:

- Overtrading
- Greed
- Not following system
- No system
- Too tight stops
- Lack of understanding
- Too emotional
- Not paying attention
- Lack of time
- Going against pros
- No goal
- Lack of plan
- Lack of confidence
- No analysis of mistakes
- Lack of capital

- Compulsion to trade
- Preconceived ideas

Sound familiar? I would imagine that you can find the reason why you don't make money somewhere in that list. I know I can find the reasons why I have gone through losing streaks.

Typically, the audience is firing these reasons at me so fast I can't keep up. It is always clear to me that they have thought about why they are losing and have a pretty clear idea. (Otherwise, why would they be sitting in this lecture?)

I think that this list can be grouped into three major categories: lack of self-discipline, lack of knowledge, and lack of capital. Some of the items fall into two categories.

I can't say that where I place each of these reasons is the final word. Some of these reasons flow between different categories. I think that not having a plan is probably a combination of a lack of discipline and knowledge, but others might argue that it is simply a lack of either of these separately. Ultimately, how the reasons for losing are categorized is almost irrelevant because what we really want to do is focus on the three main categories and how to deal with them.

The three main categories are lack of discipline, knowledge, and capital. The latter two are probably the easiest to deal with and lack of discipline is usually the hardest. Why? Because it involves a change in your character. Money and knowledge can always be acquired, but changing one's character is usually extremely difficult.

Let's talk first about the two lesser problems before going to the issue of self-discipline. I think you will soon see that self-discipline is the real key to success in trading because it permeates even the two lesser problems.

ADDRESSING A LACK OF KNOWLEDGE

Frankly, this is the easiest of the three main problems to solve. Knowledge can be acquired in many ways:

- Reading books
- Reading magazines
- Attending seminars
- Attending classes
- Finding a mentor
- Swapping information with a friend
- Watching video tapes

- Reading blogs
- Reading Web sites
- Just doing it!

It doesn't really take money to learn. Books are affordable. Blogs are free. A library card is free.

Virtually all the knowledge you need is available for free at the library. You don't need to go to a $3,000 seminar to learn all you need to know to make significant profits trading forex.

What you *do* need to know are the basics, such as contract specifications, what is a long and short, and so on. Second, you need to know some entry and exit techniques if you use technical analysis and you will need to know something about the underlying currency pair if you are going to use fundamental analysis.

In many respects, that's all you need to know. The intellectual knowledge to profitably trade forex is trivial, far less than what you know about your job.

Take another look at the list above. A lack of knowledge is not really a lack of knowledge relating to the intellectual knowledge necessary to trade but is, instead, related to the psychology of trading.

Take a look at some of the audience members' responses again:

- No system
- Lack of understanding
- No goal
- Lack of a plan
- Lack of confidence
- No analysis of mistakes
- Preconceived ideas

Only the first two are really a lack of intellectual knowledge. The rest are a lack of psychological knowledge. In fact, you can see that the vast majority of the items on the list are related more to a lack of self-discipline or a clear lack of focus.

Yes, of course it is good to be constantly learning more about trading. The more you know about trading or markets, the more likely it is that you make money. However, you can see that few people thought that they needed to know more before they could make money. The lack of knowledge is really the lack of knowledge about oneself or of one's own trading.

In general, you can see that the audience's list is really a list of psychological failures. It is a list of things that could create a profitable trading plan that are not being done. Once again, the audience knew what the problems were but were apparently helpless to do something about it.

They knew they had no goal, plan, and/or confidence but hadn't done anything to correct this potentially fatal flaw in their trading. Why not? I believe that the answer lies first in the discussion of why people trade. Perhaps—and this is likely the problem—making money is not their priority.

But let's assume that this is not the case and that they really are motivated to make money trading forex. I think then that the problem is a lack of self-discipline. Once again, they know the problem but have not conquered it. Solving these kinds of problems requires an insight into the problem, a plan to solve the problem, and the self-discipline to apply the solution.

Clearly, people have an insight into the problem or they wouldn't have listed it. That means that they now must have a plan and the self-discipline to put the plan into place. It is beyond the scope of this book to come up with a plan for each of these problems. However, the issue of self-discipline will be dealt with in great detail later.

ADDRESSING A LACK OF CAPITAL

A lack of capital means that you are overtrading and risking too much of your capital on each trade. The lack of capital may be the easiest of all the problems to solve. You must either raise more capital or risk less on each trade.

The first solution obviously requires you to either earn and save money or to allocate more of your current assets to forex trading. The second solution is easy to do as well. However, the problem comes when your account is very small, such as under $10,000. It's easy to find lots of interesting trades when your account has $250,000 but much harder when you only have $5,000.

A detailed description of money management concepts is beyond the scope of this book. However, let's assume that you risk 1 percent of your equity with every trade. This means that you can only lose $100 on each trade if you have $10,000 in your account. Clearly, there are few trades that you can enter and only risk $100.

There are several solutions. First, save and invest more money. The more money you have in the account, the more you can risk per trade. For example, using a 1 percent bet size, you could risk $200 on a $20,000 account, $500 on a $50,000 account and so on. There are obviously a lot more trade opportunities when you can risk $500 than when you risk $100.

A second alternative is to risk more per trade. For example, risk 2 percent or 3 percent of your equity on each trade. This will give you many more opportunities to make money but it will increase the risk of ruin.

Sometimes this is the only alternative. You take more risk than you should in order to play the game. However, the greater the risk you take, the greater the chance that you get wiped out. It's sort of like "double or nothing." On the other hand, prudent money management means that you are much more likely to succeed and that you are treating trading forex like a business.

Do not take this issue of bet size too lightly. I think that it is one of the most important issues there is in trading forex.

I once had a meeting with a gentleman who was very proud of his forex trading track record. He said that he had tripled his $1.5 million in the first quarter of this year. I told him that I was duly impressed but asked him how long he had been trading. He replied that he had just started at the beginning of the year. My enthusiasm shrank considerably. Of course, I was still impressed with him tripling his money but had to ask the obvious next question: "How much of your bankroll do you bet on each trade?"

He casually replied, "I like to keep the risk to a third or less of my capital." My jaw dropped. I literally couldn't believe my ears. Did he just say that he bet a third of his total bankroll on each trade? I had to ask again and he stated that this was the case. He seemed proud of his conservatism!

Well, I will tell you that he is guaranteed to be wiped out. There is no way that he will go long before he has three straight losing trades. I know that I have many of those every year.

The point: You can take greater risk than you prudently should but you are also increasing your risk of ruin.

A lot of people mistakenly think that they can't trade forex and only risk a few hundred dollars per trade. They think they need to risk at least $500 per trade and, more likely, $1,000 per trade to make money. In general, I think that this is true.

One of the great things about forex is that it is possible to open forex trading accounts with just a few hundred dollars. These accounts allow you to trade mini- and even microaccounts where the trade size is as low as $1,000 and each pip is worth just ten cents.

ADDRESSING A LACK OF SELF-DISCIPLINE

In my opinion, a lack of self-discipline is the main reason that people fail at trading. Almost every reason that people give for failing has a tie with lack of self-discipline. Plans, goals, systems, techniques, and knowledge are all useless if there is no self-discipline to apply them.

It seems to me that everybody agrees that self-discipline is the key to forex trading success. But no one shows you how to achieve it. I will attempt, in this chapter, to provide techniques for boosting self-discipline and your forex trading profits.

Why do we lack self-discipline? No one can say for certain but I believe that our own ego is the primary cause of a lack of self-discipline. We need to validate ourselves. We need to show that we are a good person. And so on and so on. Our ego has huge needs that get in the way of trading success.

I'm not saying that the ego is all bad. On the contrary. We need to have a strong ego to trade again after being beat up in the markets. We have to feel strong enough to take the psychological pressures of trading and keep going.

But the ego is also the cause of nearly all long-term trading losses, in my opinion. It's not natural to trade. We have to overcome our ego to be successful yet still allow our ego to motivate us to make money. It is a fine line between humility and egomania that we are trying to find.

In my career, I have hired many people to be traders for me. Many had little or no experience. I always looked on their resume for some indication that they had self-discipline. Had they been in the Marines or other armed forces? Had they been heavily involved in sports or gotten a degree in something like engineering, math, or physics? All of these are indications that they may have a lot of self-discipline.

It has been my experience that Marines and athletes are represented far beyond their normal representation in society in the numbers of successful traders. Why? Because it takes tremendous self-discipline to be successful in those two areas.

Notice that I do not look for people who know a lot about forex trading or have MBAs, although it is preferred that they have some knowledge of forex. I can teach the intellectual knowledge necessary to trade but it is much more difficult to teach self-discipline. However, that is exactly what I hope to do in the rest of the chapter.

Unfortunately, self-discipline is not something that can be taught. It has to come from within. Nobody can create self-discipline for you. This sounds reflexive: You must have self-discipline to acquire self-discipline. To a certain extent, this is true. This chapter will not teach you self-discipline; only you can do that. However, it is often possible to pick up techniques or tricks that can boost your self-discipline. You may find that some of the following techniques provide the impetus toward self-discipline. Some may work for you and others will fall flat.

I have used all of the techniques with success for both myself and in my teaching others to be successful traders. They may work for you. There is no magic in them. They are simply techniques for trying to enforce self-discipline in trading forex. They are designed to help you become a better trader.

Please note that I am outlining techniques. You can change them to fit your own needs and desires. Take these ideas and make them your own. They will work better for you that way.

AN EXAMPLE OF OVERCOMING THE BIZARRE TWISTS AND TURNS OF THE MIND

It's amazing what tricks the mind will play. It's as if you don't really want to make money and you look for strange ways to lose money. A good friend of mine is a perfect example.

He is arguably the smartest person I know. He has awesome intelligence and is very knowledgeable about many subjects. He decided that he wanted to be a professional trader. I showed him some techniques and he took them to another level and created his own mechanical methods. He got his quote screen all set up and was ready to trade.

I helped him open a futures account with the same broker that I used. Normally, the broker only handles institutional accounts but he decided to allow my friend to open an account with only $10,000 as a favor to me. He also allowed him to trade at institutional commission rates that are roughly half those charged by retail brokers.

Turns out that my friend proceeded to lose about 60 percent of his bankroll over the next six months. This was a terrible track record since it meant that he was losing consistently because he was able to keep his risk to below a couple of hundred dollars for each trade. That means he had a lot of losing trades. It was quite remarkable because the system he was trading had very little discretion and had such a tremendous track record while being tested.

He went back over the track record of the system during the time that he was actually trading it. Turns out that he had lost 60 percent but that the system was profitable. In other words, he was not actually following the system. He was not executing the trades according to the signals.

It turns out that he was intimidated by calling an institutional broker and only putting in a one- or two-lot order. He felt that he was wasting their time since they were used to dealing in larger quantities and that they were doing it only as a concession for me. The brokers had never complained but my friend had projected a problem where none existed. He would hesitate before entering a trade and ended up missing many trades and creating a huge slippage problem.

The solution was obvious! Shift his account to a retail broker that charged twice as much and gave poorer service!

By shifting his account to a retail broker, he felt that he wasn't bothering anybody and could go back to focusing on the market instead of his relationship with his broker. He was getting worse fills and paying twice as much in commissions but was starting to make money. He had found the bizarre little problem in his mind that was stopping him from making money. The good news is that he could easily solve the problem.

TREAT TRADING AS EDUCATION

Rather than think of trading as a means of making or losing money, think of what you can learn from each trade and from trading in general. Think of trading as going to university but with a pop quiz every day.

Focus on what you are learning as you go through the trading experience. Every time you exit a position, look at the trade and try to identify what you learned rather than how much money you made or lost. Ask yourself, did I analyze the commodity correctly? Did I understand the driving forces that caused it to move? What should I learn before my next trade? Did I follow my plan? Did I enter the trade well? Did I exit the trade well? What were my emotions while I entered/exited the trade? What could I have done better? What did I do well? What did I do poorly?

Your answers should give you some idea of the kinds of questions you can ask yourself to further your education. The point is to focus like a laser beam on learning, not on your profit and loss.

Normally, people focus on how much money they made or lost. But, in a way, that is irrelevant. Money will be made or lost on every trade. The real issue is whether your bankroll is increasing over a longer period of time, say a month, a quarter, or even a year. It is highly unlikely that you will make money over the long run if you do not constantly improve as a trader, particularly if you are not currently a profitable trader.

I have been a professional trader for more than 20 years and have only one year that was even close to a losing year. But I still spend a tremendous amount of time trying to improve my craft.

One of the best techniques for improving trading is to keep a trading journal. This is a simple book where you enter every day such information as what trades you are considering, why you are entering the trade and why exit, and other information about your trades. You should also put your emotions and reactions in the journal. In particular, you should put down your emotional state of mind when you are trading. The idea is to take an emotional snapshot of yourself each day. Are you feeling cool, calm, and collected? Then you are far more likely to make money that day. Are you feeling anxious? Then you are far more likely to lose money that day.

One of my primary reasons for buying *Commodity Trading Consumer Research* (CTCR) from Bruce Babcock was that it gave me the opportunity to interview and learn from some of the best traders in the world and it also allowed me access to books, systems, and other products so that I could learn more.

If I do not constantly strive to learn then I will be caught when market conditions change. I used mechanical trading systems extensively back in the 1970s and 1980s. I got very nervous about the efficacy of them in the late 1980s when I saw Mint (a very large commodity money manager) acquire $1 billion under management. They were the first to achieve that amount of money. They used a standard trend-following method based roughly on a 40-day moving average.

I felt that if there was a company with a billion dollars under management then that particular style would find it very difficult to make money because it had so much buying and selling power that it *was* the market. It would dominate the market so much that it would not be able to make money. There would not be enough liquidity in most markets to allow it to diversify.

Remember, Mint was only the tip of the iceberg. It had a billion dollars but there were lots of other plain vanilla trend followers in the market at the same time. After all, I was one of them. I wasn't doing anything special in my trend-following systems.

I felt that the returns to trend-following systems would degrade because there was too much money flowing into the market all at the same time and that the profits from the systems would not be as high as they had been in the past. I decided that I would have to change my method of entry and exit. You see, I use fundamentals to determine the direction that I want to trade in and used mechanical systems for the entry and exit. If mechanical systems were being overused then I would have to learn an entirely different method of entry and exit. I ended up switching to a classic chart analysis method.

It turns out that trend-following systems did, in fact, go through a period of poor performance. (I think that the amount of money under management of trend-following systems has been reduced, as a percentage of the total amount under management, and that trend-following systems will again produce good results.)

The point is that I had to be aware that what I had been doing may not work in the future and that I had to learn a new skill or I was out of business. I had to make sure that I had backup skills in case my current skills were no longer being rewarded by the market. Conditions change: Make sure that you are prepared for it.

A focus on constant learning is essential if you are going to be in this game for a long time. Market conditions change; you must be alert to those changes and have a depth of knowledge to draw from if you need to change your trading strategies or tactics.

I believe that trading success is built on the excellent execution of a few fundamentals. You don't need to get fancy, just focus on the fundamentals. I think that you will find that most of your losing trades come from breaking a few fundamental rules, such as not placing and sticking to a preset stop loss level.

Switching the focus onto learning and away from profits and losses helps to reduce the emotions associated with trading. You can look at each trade much more objectively because you almost don't care if you made or lost money. In a curious way, you might even "enjoy" losing trades more than winning trades because you can usually learn more from the experience.

Notice that this point of view helps to promote good trading practices. Remember, you should be noting everything you did right in the trade as well as what you did wrong. This will reinforce behavior that produces profitable trades. In a way, the definition of a *good trade* changes. A trade becomes a good trade when you learn something new, not only when it makes money.

Notice how powerful a different mind-set can be. Making or losing money on a given trade becomes no big deal. Instead, you try to analyze your trading dispassionately to see how to improve. You are almost forced to be objective.

The flip side is that a tremendous pressure will be taken off of you. You are no longer judged (by yourself) by the success or failure of your last trade. The pressure of success is replaced by the pressure to improve as a trader. That is a much better pressure to feel and will lead to better trading and more profits. It is much better to kick yourself for not learning as much as you could than to kick yourself for losing more money. You will be motivated to study your trading rather than feeling sorry for yourself or angry with yourself.

Focusing on your own trading will also keep you from relying on others for your profits. It is possible to use systems and ideas from others profitably, but you will never learn anything. In the final analysis that is okay, but few people have the self-discipline to simply follow a system. Most people want to have some input into the trading decision. This ties back to the ego problem.

You don't need to get fancy in your trading. Just execute a few basics well. Your education-based feedback mechanism will show you what you are doing well. I have a friend who only trades reversal days. I keep trying to get him to try another method but he says to me that he is making a living doing this so why screw up a good thing?

The bottom line is that changing your focus from making money to constantly learning will sharply reduce your stress level, keep you focused on learning how to make more money, and increase your self-discipline.

STRESS-FREE TRADING

One of the keys to profitable trading is to reduce stress. Most of this chapter is about techniques to reduce or eliminate stress. Stress is unhealthy and gets in the way of profitable trading. One of the keys to reducing stress is to think in terms of probabilities rather than in absolutes.

Think of the stress when you put on a trade and naturally think, "I'm going to make money on this trade." That is what we normally think when we put on a trade. Actually, we should be thinking, "I'm probably going to make money on this trade."

The first statement will create a lot of stress if you have a losing trade. You internally predicted something that didn't come true. You were wrong. You don't want to be wrong. You feel stress. The second statement creates far less stress if you have a losing trade. You predicted that you would make money but you also predicted that there was a fair chance that you would lose money. You were sorta right and sorta wrong. Big deal.

I turn a profit on less than 50 percent of my trades but I am still a money-making trader. So my internal prediction is, "I'll probably lose money on this trade but I will make money on my trading." How much less stress is that? I'm actually predicting that I will lose money on this particular trade so I feel like a smart guy when I do have that losing trade.

As traders, we must be both humble and bold at the same time. We must be humble and realize that we will have many losing trades, hundreds of them, thousands of them. Get used to it. It's no big deal.

At the same time, we must be bold so that we have the courage and discipline to get up tomorrow and put on a new trade. We must also be consistent and persistent. We must be a machine. A money machine.

We have a winning trade. Then continue to execute flawlessly. We have a losing trade. Then continue to execute flawlessly. We have five winning trades in a row or five losing trades in a row. Then continue to execute flawlessly.

Don't get frustrated. Don't get bored. Don't even get excited. You are a money machine. You are the casino. Execute. Execute. Execute.

BE THE CASINO

In my trading classes, I ask my students how many of them have been to a casino and gambled. The majority will raise their hands. I then ask those who consistently make money to leave their hands in the air.

All the hands go down.

It is always astounding to me to see that so many people go to a casino and gamble basically knowing that they will lose. I ask them why they go. They say that it is the thrill that they *might* win. Might! Of course I chide them for this lack of discipline. But then I ask them if they think the casino makes money every year. Of course, the answer is yes. Casinos rarely go belly up. I can see the students' eyes light up.

The reality is that we want to emulate casinos in our trading business. They only play games that they have an edge in. We want to do the same. We want to only use trading methods that make money. The casino is never foolish enough to let you play a game that you could win over the long run. We must do the same.

Just because the casino has an edge still doesn't mean that it is guaranteed to make money. It still must execute flawlessly to ensure profits. Imagine the owner of a casino getting up one day and deciding that he didn't like the blackjack dealers and appointed me and you to do the dealing this week. Well, I imagine that you are like me and don't know how to deal blackjack professionally. Further imagine that he decides that he is bored with sweeping the floors and decides to stop it. And then he notices that he has had a losing trade for three straight months by having to pay for electricity to light the casino. He flinches on the fourth month because he doesn't want another losing trade and doesn't pay the bill.

This casino is clearly going out of business soon. Yet the casino has to deal with many of the same issues that we do as professional traders. It must only play games in which it has an edge and it must execute flawlessly. In my example, the casino owner was not executing flawlessly.

My examples may seem absurd but they are not so absurd when we individual traders examine our own behavior. We do the same kinds of dumb behavior all the time. When you sit down at a roulette table, does the casino owner get fearful? Does he flinch and stop you from gambling? More important, does he get upset when he loses a spin? Or two? Or three?

No! The bottom line is that the casino owner doesn't care what happens on the next spin or the next or the next. What he cares about is the next 1,000 spins or the next million spins. He knows that the next spin is not relevant to his profitability at the end of the month. He could not care less what happens. He knows that he has an edge and he wants to work it as much as possible.

Does he knows that he will often lose three hands of blackjack in a row? Of course. He also knows that he will lose 10 in a row every so often. And he even knows that once in a very long time he will lose 100 hands in a row.

But he also knows that the inverse will happen. Even more often. He knows that losing streaks will happen. That is the price of getting the suckers in to play the game. The casino owners don't freak out when streaks happen. They don't fret about telling the wife or think that it reflects badly on themselves as a person. They simply deal the cards again. They know they will win in the end and their job is to execute flawlessly so that their edge will come to them and they will make money for the casino.

I urge you to mentally think of yourself as the casino. If you are in a quandary over what to do or if you are feeling some emotion related to trading, ask yourself what a casino owner would do or feel.

DEVELOPING YOUR TRADING PLAN

Perhaps the most powerful technique for increasing self-discipline is the use of a trading plan and the attendant postmortem technique. I am going to go into detail about this technique and will show real examples of trading plans.

Traders lose money mostly from making stupid mistakes. They forget to put in the stop because they will do it tomorrow. They don't know the right contract size. They like the way the stochastics are acting but completely ignore the breakdown on the chart. And so on. In other words, they simply forget to take a look at something that they know they should look at.

I think that the two main reasons for not looking at something that you should are:

1. Not paying attention due to a busy schedule or not caring
2. Not wanting to confuse your opinion with facts

I firmly believe that the consistent use of a trading plan will overcome these two problems. I further believe that the trading plan is the second most important part of a trade, after money management. The actual entry and exit techniques are secondary. Most traders will find this statement hard to accept but most profitable traders, even if they do not use a trading plan, will agree with me. There are several reasons why.

Without proper monitoring of information, you will drown in a flood of information. With a trading plan, all the relevant fundamental and technical indicators can be stored in one spot. It will allow you to outline a scenario of the expectations for the future. In addition, it provides a place for the exact entry and exit points to be delineated and necessary money management principles to be applied.

One of the important features of the trading plan is that it is devised before the money is risked. Traders are typically far less emotional about a trade before the money is committed. Typically, traders lose their objectivity when they are on the firing line and money is committed.

The trading plan also helps to educate you. After a trade, you can go over your trading plans and evaluate what actually happened. This is called the postmortem. You have an opportunity to examine how accurate the pretrade analysis was and discover areas of weakness in your own education or insights. Often, investors will realize that certain facets of their trading technique have been over- or underestimated. They think that a particular technique is doing well when, in fact, it is doing poorly. Traders can refer back to the trading plan while in the trade to determine whether things are going as planned and whether there have been significant changes that will affect the analysis that led to initiating the position. The trading plan thus becomes a rudder for the average speculator, who tends to trade like a rudderless ship. When investors are forced to commit thoughts to paper before initiating the trade, their thoughts must be more logical and coherent. The record of the thoughts before the trade is initiated provides a useful insight for future growth.

The use of a trading plan is also a viable way of reducing mental fatigue and anxiety. The trading plan is a record of the thoughts of the trader before the trade is initiated. It represents a calmer, detached state of mind than will exist when money is on the line. Traders who have committed money based on a rational trading plan will be able to refer back to that trading plan and use it as a touchstone of calm.

FILLING OUT THE PLAN

Many people believe a trading plan is a waste of time. Filling out a trading plan takes time but is probably a major time-saver in the final analysis. Most average speculators will spend a tremendous amount of time and valuable energy watching the market on a tick-by-tick basis. This seems to be based on the psychological concept that if they do not watch the market it will go against them. This constant staring at a screen is an incredibly time-consuming activity. There is a major loss of energy when a trader's mind is unfocused. The trading plan enforces a certain discipline, requiring that traders specify the entry and exit points and the method of stop placement before the trade is initiated. This means that traders can enter entry and exit points once a day rather than staring at a screen all day long looking for clues to the future direction of the market. The trading plan will reduce traders' impulsive behavior when prices get close to entry or exit points. There are often nagging second thoughts about a trade when prices begin to get close to the entry point. This doubt about the trade is really a form of self-doubt and often occurs when traders are not using a trading plan. The use of a trading plan releases traders from having to watch the market on a micro level. The time saved can be spent analyzing the markets and acquiring more knowledge.

Remember, the main point of a trading plan is to help increase discipline. A written plan is far superior to a mental plan. It is extremely difficult for the human mind to take into account all possible factors in a rational manner when they are not written down. A mental trading plan tends to become a plan composed of wishful thinking rather than hard critical analysis. Furthermore, the written plan provides the opportunity for traders to conduct a postmortem analysis on the trade (we will discuss this later in detail). It is probably easier for traders to acquire the discipline to fill out the trading plan than it is to acquire the psychological discipline necessary to function without a trading plan.

You should fill out a trading plan whenever you have an idea that you are thinking of trading. You may see a chart pattern or read an article in the paper and think that there is something worthwhile to follow upon. You may become bullish on a particular forex pair because of a particular analysis you have done. You should then fill out the trading plan before entering the position because it will enforce your self-discipline.

A trading plan can be in any form. It can be a form that is filled out or a narrative in your journal or a line on a spreadsheet. Whatever works for you.

I recommend that you use a form or journal if you are incorporating fundamentals in your trading. This will be in conjunction with the technical techniques you learned in this book. I suggest that traders analyze each trade from both perspectives. The elimination of one technique will leave the trader trading with one eye. The use of both techniques combined provides a synergy. It also allows traders to eliminate absurd trades.

Of course, most traders trade only with technicals. So simply create a trading plan on a spreadsheet. Just make sure that you include a Notes section where you put the postmortem that we are going to talk about in the next section.

To me, it is critical to put down the technique that you are using to enter, add, or exit the position. For example, you can say that you are entering on a channel breakout and exiting on a channel breakout. On my sheet, I simply have CB as a column and I put the current entry and exit price on the sheet.

I have been trading for many years and I am always amazed at how much better my original plan is than what I end up doing. I change my plan midstream far too often. I go back and see what would have happened if I had simply stuck to my original plan and the original plan is nearly always better. Why? Because it is devised in an atmosphere of calm and calculated reason rather than in the heat of battle. It gives me a clearer picture of the future and the best way to play it. It also creates a better atmosphere for self-discipline. Here's the plan, now stick to it.

One of the key reasons why I recommend this approach to nonprofessional investors is that it saves time. You write the plan once and do not deviate, no matter what happens in the future. This usually means that you don't have to call your broker to change orders very often and you certainly don't have to reanalyze the market. Okay, perhaps you should reanalyze, but only after several weeks or even months have gone by so that you don't spend too much time.

Some investors will say that this is ridiculous and that not taking into consideration changes in market conditions is foolish and will lead to losses. It turns out that this is not necessarily true. It sounds good in theory but doesn't work in fact.

I undertook a study at a trading firm that I worked at back in the 1980s. I asked the traders to make a trading plan for every trade. Sometimes, there would be a significant news item at some point during the trade. Let's say that we are sitting on a profit in the trade and the news causes the market to dip. Should we take into account this fresh piece of information or stick to the original trading plan? At the time, it seemed clear to me that we should take into account the new information. Why should we trade using information that is weeks old when we can use the freshest info possible?

Based on my study, we would have made more money 80 percent of the time by sticking with the original trading plan rather than ignoring that plan and trading off the new information. I think this result occurs because we lose objectivity once we are in a position. Our minds are blown. We can't evaluate the new information rationally. We can't use that information in a rational way. On the other hand, we were calm, cool, and collected when we put together our trading plan. We had no emotional skin in the game.

What happens is that you second-guess yourself and don't retain as much self-discipline. You read another article that makes you second-guess your deeply thought-out analysis in the trading plan and tend to pull out of the trade based on just a little bit of new evidence. I wouldn't have a big problem if you go back and do the whole analysis from scratch if you read a new article and think that the conditions have changed enough to exit the position. But few people have the self-discipline to do this. It is hard enough to get people to do the initial trading plan.

The basic problem is that investors second-guess their plans in the heat of battle without the benefit of a calm, reasoned approach. This means that they will shade all of their analysis toward what their heart or guts want rather than what their brain wants.

I have trained many traders over the years and few trades work out better by overriding the original plan. Of course, if you have a position on for many weeks, you may want to start your analysis all over. There will be enough new information that needs to be processed. However, you may want to even consider exiting the position temporarily to make sure that you have sufficient self-discipline while you do the new analysis. The main thing to remember is that you will likely need to change the exit rule. That old trend line might not be valid anymore. Still, be careful not to change the original plan too much.

THE IMPORTANCE OF A POSTMORTEM

This is one of the truly great techniques for attaining greater self-discipline, increasing your skills as a trader, and focusing more on educating yourself. I am a big fan of postmortems and have written about them for more than 25 years.

A *postmortem* is taking each of your trades and tearing it apart from the perspective of seeing what you can learn. This is easiest if you are using a trading plan because the plan is a record of what you were thinking and you will not have to rely on your faulty memory to figure out what you were thinking.

The first thing to look at is the trading plan and see how your analysis held up. When you said that the stochastics were bearish, did the market go down? Were your milestones the correct milestones to consider? Did you correctly identify the driving fundamentals?

As far as self-discipline is concerned, the key factor is the action section of the trading plan. Did you follow your plan? Did you enter and exit the trade when you said that you would and use the techniques that you said you would? Grade yourself hard because it is here that your lack of self-discipline will really show up. It is here that most traders fail. They typically enter the trade correctly but fail to use the exit technique outline in the plan. They either panic and jump out too soon or get stubborn and don't get out until it's too late.

Take the trading plan and use a red pen to grade yourself. Mark on the plan where you succeeded and where you failed. It's important to see where you succeeded because you want to promote good habits in your trading. You want to see where you failed so that you can reduce the propensity to do it again.

Take the initial trading plan and your postmortem and file them away. Then, every several months, take them out and read through them. You will find it fascinating to see a living record of your trading.

Look very closely for patterns of success and failure. For example, I studied Elliott Wave analysis for months. I initiated many trades largely based on my Elliott Wave analysis. I gave up on it when I studied my postmortems and realized that I rarely had a winning trade using Elliott Wave. That doesn't mean that Elliott Wave is not a valid form of analysis but it does mean that I couldn't apply the concepts and make money.

You will start to see areas where your analysis is consistently leading you to profitable trades or where your behavior is leading you to losing trades and so on. Look to study the profitability of your techniques and, more important, where you succeeded or failed from a self-discipline point of view.

The postmortem is a key to becoming a better trader. You can continually refine your abilities as a trader. Let's say that you are trading five different methods. You go out and start to trade a sixth method. After a year, you sit down and throw out the worst of the techniques and trade the top five for the coming year. Of course, you will want to now find a new sixth system to test for the next year. Perhaps the new system is better than one of the old ones. Perhaps not. You will gain incremental profit if the new system is better than just one of the old ones. Multiply this concept for the rest of your trading career and you can see that this can add dramatically to your profits each year.

Now imagine that you have increased your annual profits by replacing inferior systems with superior systems each year. Now compound those gains.

Again.

And again.

Do you see how powerful this substitution technique is for building serious wealth in your life?

Notice how the postmortem forces you to grade yourself and your techniques. It forces you to learn more about trading. It forces you to become more focused on education and self-discipline. You will feel less pressure to make money and more pressure to become a better trader. You will either unlock the key to becoming a successful trader or you will find the reason why you cannot be a profitable trader.

THE BOTTOM LINE

This completes our exploration of how to stop being a losing forex trader. I covered what is, in my opinion, the most important issue: self-discipline. I showed you proven techniques that can boost your self-discipline. I showed you concepts to help you understand your motivations for trading and how they impact your profitability.

I believe that a combination of the techniques outlined in this chapter with tight money and risk management can turn any trader from showing losses to at least breaking even, and that is a remarkable turn of events when you consider that roughly 90 percent of traders lose money. You should be able to get into the top decile of all traders with these techniques.

CHAPTER 10

Putting It All Together

I have presented a comprehensive program for profits. It includes all the essential elements for creating massive profits for the rest of your life:

- Tools and concepts for creating the right psychology for trading success
- Specific techniques and methods for identifying entry and exit points
- Risk management actions to ensure that you are protecting yourself from loss and maximizing profit

Each element of the program supports the others, so it will be difficult to make money and cut out one of the key elements. They all need to be in place to really make money in the forex market. This is not to say that each element isn't a stand-alone idea that can improve your current results, but the synergy between them is a massive bonus.

DIVERSIFYING TO REDUCE RISK

One of the critical components of the program is the concept of diversifying through time. We all know that diversifying is a way to reduce risk. But when everyone talks about diversification, they are talking about diversifying the instruments that you trade. A classic example is to not invest in just five stocks but have at least 30 stocks in your portfolio to diversify your risk. And, in fact, the more stocks you have in your portfolio, the less volatility of returns you will have.

However, there are other ways to diversify to lower risk. For example, you can diversify through time. Having different methods trade at different time periods will reduce the risk in your portfolio even with the same number of instruments. I have given you methods that will trade on short-term time frames as well as longer time frames. For example, trend analysis tends to be looking at the market over a several-week time frame while channel breakout looks at 55 days or almost three months. Then add in the short-term methods like inside days and you have a lot of different time frames covered.

You can have one method long and another short. That has the effect of reducing the volatility of returns in your portfolio because sideways markets can get the various methods going in different directions. This particularly happens with the pattern recognition techniques.

It cannot be stressed enough: It is important to execute flawlessly each part of the program, particularly the psychological and risk management rules. A breakdown in discipline will put your equity at risk.

Even though I am telling you that all of these elements fit together, you should still trade each of the entry and exit methods as if the other methods didn't exist. In other words, you should trade trend analysis with laser precision as if channel breakouts didn't exist.

USE A MENTAL CHECKLIST

I look at my charts every day and simply go through the mental process of checking for new trades and changes to existing trades method by method. "Here's EUR/USD. In a trade already using channel breakout? If yes, do I need to change my stop? If no, do I need to change the entry stop? In a trade using trend analysis? If yes, do I need to change my stop? If no, can I enter a trade? If yes, then put in entry stop. If no, then go on to the next pair." And so on. At no point do I look at another method to see what it is doing when I'm looking at one method. This constant monitoring can get us all the advantages of diversifying through time.

Note that you can use the multiunit tactic on all methods. I only talked about it briefly in the book, but you can use it on every technique.

Some traders will only have small accounts and not be able to execute every trade of every method even with a mini-account. One suggestion is to pick just one technique and execute that one flawlessly. Pick the one that fits your psychology the best to ensure the highest discipline. Add additional methods as your bankroll expands. Another possibility is to shift to a micro-account and trade more methods. This is preferred because it helps to diversify the risk.

HOW TO TRADE ONLY ONE METHOD

Which system should you use if you can only trade one? I guess I would pick the channel breakout for the position trading and inside days for the day trading. I think they are the best in terms of keeping risk tight yet having a large profit potential.

A final comment on tying the various techniques together is what I call the holistic or weight of evidence method. The basic idea is that you trade according to the weight of the evidence. Let's say you are using Conqueror, channel breakout, and trend analysis. You will go long when the majority of those techniques are bullish and short when the majority are bearish. You will always use the tightest stop of the three.

Now note that it is possible that you will be flat the market on occasion. Let's assume that all systems are flat to start. The trend analysis then gives a buy signal to go long and we enter a buy order that gets filled. We are now long with a stop when the trend analysis tells us to get long. We then get a sell signal from the channel breakout that gets filled before we are stopped out on the trend analysis. You take that trade as well, which gets you flat the market. Technically, you are now long and short with protective stops in the market. Basically, you will get long again when the channel breakout trades get stopped out or get short if the trend analysis gets stopped out.

The market trades along for a while and the Conqueror gets long on the same day that the channel breakout gets stopped out. You are now long three contracts with three different stop losses. You continue doing exactly this method so that your position will vary from three short to three long and everything in between. You will therefore be the longest or the shortest when the market is the strongest or the weakest. And that is exactly what you want to be.

Smaller investors will also find the weight of evidence to be useful. In this method, you don't go long until, say, all three methods turn bullish. In other words, you would wait until two methods are long and then you put in an order to enter long on the signal for the third method. You then place a protective stop at the point that the closest method would get stopped out. In other words, you may be entering on a trend analysis entry stop but exiting on a Conqueror exit stop. In other words, you will only be trading one contract but you wouldn't be entering until all three methods are long and are exiting the position when just one of the methods exits. By using these techniques, the smaller trader can gain exposure to the market without entering very many trades.

THE BOTTOM LINE

All of the techniques, risk management, and psychology integrate into a total package for making money. It is a powerful combination that can create massive profits for you, and it is best if you use all the techniques because that will reduce the risk the most.

It will also give you the most chances to create profit.

Key Insights for Maximizing Your Trading Profits

T rading forex is close to the ideal business. Unlike many other businesses, you don't have to deal with the usual problems, such as:

Employees
Employment taxes
Regulations
Rent
Health insurance

The list goes on and on. Those of you who have run a business know all about the many issues.

Most businesses have employees. The advantage of employees is that they can leverage your business. They can do things you can't or don't want to do. That is about all they are good for. On the other hand, you have to pay them. You have to act as priest, mother, and psychiatrist to them. You have to pay taxes on them. They can be a pain in the neck. So a big advantage to being a forex trader is that you don't have to have any employees.

In most areas of the world, trading profits are tax free. That alone almost makes it worthwhile to be a trader. You don't need any inventory. That means that you never have to have sales to dump your inventory that doesn't sell. You can open your trading business for 24 hours a day or 15 minutes a day. And you get to pick which 15 minutes! Unlike the traditional business with all of its problems, trading is far more attractive.

The only drawback is that you still have to have capital to start your business. In trading, you can actually open a micro-forex account with as little as $250! Of course you won't make much money by starting with only $250 but you can ensure that you are a good trader before investing more capital. You will be able to learn while risking very little.

Perhaps one of the best aspects of trading is that you can do it just about anywhere in the world. All you need is a decent Internet connection. I've written parts of this book in Singapore, Malaysia, Hong Kong, Los Angeles, and Belize! Only in the remote island in Belize did I really have a problem with my Internet connection that made it slightly difficult. Everywhere else was easy!

To me, the greatest attribute of trading forex as a professional is that I can do it anywhere and anytime in the world. I am not constrained by the normal bounds of a business. This means that my trading supports my life, not my life supporting my trading. Never forget why you are trading. Yes, trading can be enjoyable in itself, though many find it stressful and not enjoyable. But we are usually trading to achieve a goal other than trading for trading's sake. We are probably looking for freedom in our life. Perhaps it is the freedom to live in different parts of the world. Perhaps it is the freedom from financial worry. Perhaps you want to help your kids through school or boost your retirement.

Whatever it is, trading should be a big part in helping you to achieve. It should not be a job or a big stress or a problem in your life. It should be a servant that is there to create a better life for you.

ALWAYS REMEMBER THAT TRADING IS A BUSINESS

I have heard for many years about traders who will spend weeks analyzing the decision to buy a $100 power tool but only five minutes on risking $10,000 trading forex. To me this is an amazing fact. Why will people be so cavalier about trading? Why don't they spend the time and energy that it demands?

Starting a business is hard. Many if not most fail. But the failure rate on forex trading is much higher. Credible estimates put the failure rate at about 90 percent. One reason is that people, deep down, do not take trading seriously. You can buy and sell so easily that it doesn't have the appearance of being hard to do. Every book and guru out there talks about how easy it is to make money if you just follow their easy steps.

I have seen many successful people founder on the shoals of trading. Doctors are a classic example of highly educated people with tremendous discipline who are typically terrible traders. For whatever reason, they do not bring the skills they have in medicine to trading. I don't mean to pick on doctors because I see it in just about everyone. Successful businessmen turn into drunken sailors when they sit down in front of a trading screen.

Do not fall into this trap.

Do all the normal things you should do if you run a business. You should be disciplined. You should be very risk averse. You should be conservative. You should think deeply before committing capital. You should look before you leap. You know the drill. Check out books about running businesses and follow their advice. I suggest that you even write a business plan about your new business. Writing such a plan could help you focus your mind. You should have an idea of where you are going before you set off into the unknown.

There is an old trading expression: "The market will do what it has to do to screw you." A plan will go a long way to negating that.

KEEP GOOD RECORDS

One key way that you can run your new trading business more professionally is to keep good records. One of the main psychological problems that I see all the time is that traders lie to themselves. I've seen many traders who cannot remember their losing trades and think that they are more profitable than they really are. I've also seen the complete opposite, where traders cannot remember their winning trades and think they are more unprofitable than they really are!

It doesn't really matter why this is but it is a rather perplexing factor. People apparently want to deceive themselves in their trading. But we must be very realistic if we are to be a profitable trader. We cannot lie to ourselves. Good record keeping is a good start for this.

There are two main reasons for keeping good records of our trading:

1. Accountability and analysis
2. Constant improvement

I advocate using at least several systems. We need to keep track of their results. We need to know the total profitability, the number of winners, the number of losers, the average size of the winning trades, and the average size of the losers as a bare minimum of information. This information can be easily keyed into a spreadsheet for analysis. I also strongly suggest keeping track of the reason why you entered and exited the trade as well as adding a column of notes.

You can now start to do some serious analysis armed with this information.

A shoe store would keep track of sales of the various models that it sells. You need to keep track of the stats for each of the methods you are using. This allows you to monitor their performance. You will want to be able to see what the profitability is compared with your expectations. Let at least six months or thirty trades go by before you start your evaluation. You want to get a very good and extensive sample before you start your analysis.

It is beyond the scope of this book to really go into the analysis of the records you are keeping on your methods. I recommend Bob Pardo's book *The Evaluation and Optimization of Trading Strategies* (John Wiley & Sons, 2008). Let me just highlight and expand on his excellent book.

Of course, the most important thing to look at is the net profitability. You want to make sure that the profitability of the method is within your expectations. In fact, you want to make sure that all parameters of the method are within your expectations. If they are, then continue to trade even if unprofitable. If they are not, then it is time to look further.

If the method is unprofitable but within your expectations, then the unprofitability is probably simply a matter of bad luck rather than bad trading. Keep trading the method for another six months and then reexamine. If a method is unprofitable for a year, it is certainly time to put it on the shelf and stop trading it until you have looked under the hood and made sure that it is still a good method.

One of the main reasons for keeping good records is to make your methods accountable. I want you to keep track of the profitability of the methods I've taught you in this book. It is important that you understand how profitable they are and how they operate. For example, 20-Day Momentum is a method that has few winning trades but they are usually very large. On the other hand, the inside days method has far more winning trades but the winning trades are much smaller.

It is useful to understand the profile of each method. For example, perhaps the lack of winning trades in 20-Day Momentum is difficult for you to handle emotionally. You should probably not trade it then because you will likely not have very high discipline. You are probably better off sticking to methods with higher win percentages.

In addition, you will want to keep good records so that you can execute the Kelly Method well. That powerful method requires a good deal of solid information before you can really implement it. Keeping good records is necessary to really make money there.

An extension of this idea is the idea of constant improvement. In this case, you are using the information from the record keeping to constantly enhance your profits.

What I recommend is this. Let's say you are using five methods. Add a sixth to the mix and trade the six methods for a year. At the end of the year, drop the worst-performing method and add a new method as the sixth method. What will happen is that you will be constantly improving your trading performance by relentlessly throwing out the worst-performing method and keeping the top five. The changes to your performance over years will be dramatic. You should not be surprised to see your performance increase by 10 percent per year for many years. That means that you could earn 40 percent this year and 44 percent next year. In ten years, you will be making vastly more money than you were at the beginning.

This is a unique concept that is rarely spoken about in trading but it is key to making massive amounts of money.

DON'T PAPER TRADE

I know, I know. This is a very controversial stand. Virtually everybody tells you to paper trade for six months to a year before you actually put money into the market.

I'm completely the opposite. I give seminars around the world. They are usually given over the weekend. I tell my students that I really want them to start trading on Monday! Naturally they are shocked. They expect to paper trade for a long time first.

I don't like paper trading because it doesn't address the real issues of trading, which are psychology and risk management. Everybody can trade reasonably well with paper money. But few can trade well in the real world.

Proponents of paper trading suggest that it allows the trader to practice the techniques before making a mistake in the real world that could cause real financial loss. True. But I recommend back-testing instead. In this case, you go back a year or more on a chart and manually go through day after day as if you were trading that time period in a real-time manner. You record your trades, thus building up a track record. Most important, you can get a year's worth of practice on five pairs in about an hour instead of a year! Back-testing provides all the value of paper trading but in a microscopic amount of time. You will also gain a lot of confidence in the methods in a very quick time. You will see the missed profits you would have made in the prior year and want to start trading right away. You can easily back-test a method on five pairs in about an hour. That means you will have five years of trading experience crammed into an hour.

After back-testing, you will have practice and confidence in a short period of time. Now you should start trading in the real world. However, I recommend that you start out trading with miniscule risk, perhaps only 0.25 percent. Trade with this incredibly low risk for several months.

Get your psychological feet wet without taking much risk. You will have to confront your psychology when you trade money, even if it is minor.

Will you make mistakes trading that will cost you money? Probably. But the amount of money will be hardly worth mentioning. At the same time, you will be gaining valuable insights and experience as a trader rather than a poseur trader. Use back-testing instead. You will make much faster progress and more money sooner than waiting for months while you paper trade.

MODEL WINNERS, NOT LOSERS

Try to find winning traders and watch and learn from them. Find out what makes them a winner and model that. Don't talk to your loser friends! Don't listen to everybody who is going to tell you that you can't make money in the markets.

Take a lot of time and try to find someone who has been making money in the markets for some time and see what they do and don't do. Most forex traders are losers so this is going to be difficult. Most gurus are losers as well. Most people who sell systems and books are losers. Don't take the fact that they wrote a book as proof that they know anything about trading. (In fact, don't take my word for it either! Go and back test all the ideas in this book to prove to yourself that they work! I challenge you!)

AVOID BOREDOM

I was interviewed in *Technical Analysis of Stocks & Commodities* magazine a number of years ago. One answer that I gave surprised them. They asked me what my biggest problem as a trader was.

I told them boredom!

They were shocked; nobody had ever suggested that. Everybody else thought that trading was exciting.

In the mid-1990s I had the opportunity to train some traders from a Korean bank. I had six traders for six months, then a second group of six traders for six months, and a final group of six traders for six months. For the first group, I brought in guest lecturers to give the students a strong grounding in all aspects of trading. One guest lecturer was a very experienced trader using Elliott Wave analysis. For those of you who are not familiar with Elliott Wave, the basic concept is that the market moves in a five-wave pattern with, in a bullish configuration, the first, third, and fifth waves going up and the second and fourth waves declining. The third wave is the biggest and most powerful wave of them all. So the Holy Grail for

Elliotticians is to try to buy the bottom of the second wave looking to ride the huge third wave up.

I let my guest lecturer do his lecture with my students and came back into the room after his lecture. I asked a series of pointed questions to make sure that the students had gotten a good idea of Elliott Wave. At one point, I asked him if he was a profitable trader. Imagine my surprise and shock when he said that he wasn't. Further, he said that he was never really a profitable trader. I was partially shocked because I thought that he had been profitable all these years that I had known him.

But then he burst out, "Well, at least what I'm doing isn't boring like the way Courtney trades!"

Turns out that he loved the feeling of catching that Wave Two dip and watching the Wave Three bull move. Problem was that he couldn't do that very often and was a losing trader.

I plead guilty to the fact that following the ideas in this book is not exciting. I'll go farther and say that most of you will find my way of trading boring. I make no excuses. I want trading to be boring, but profitable. I want trading to be something you do for 15 minutes a day and then go on with your life.

If trading is exciting, then you are likely to get excited, and getting excited is usually a recipe for losing money. Think of the casino owner. Does he get excited when you sit down at the blackjack table? No, he is bored. He already knows the outcome of the exercise. Contrast this with the gambler. The gambler is there to get excited. Gamblers know that they are likely to lose money but they are there to get excited. They have a chance of winning and the process of gambling is exciting. But who wins? The guy who is bored or the guy who is excited?

Boredom is one of my personal issues with trading. Here is how I have overcome it.

One advantage that I have is that I am a scientific person. So what I have done is created a structure that turns my boredom into increasing profits. What I do is to take a technique that I am using and then try to create an enhancement to it. Let's say that I take channel breakouts and then come up with an enhancement that says that I will only take trades in months with blue moons. I then turn on my scientific brain. I now have a control method, channel breakouts, and an experimental method, Blue Moon Channel Breakouts.

I now put on both trades from both methods. I flawlessly execute both methods. I am excited every day to see which method is "winning" the battle. Which method will be more profitable and/or has less risk. I keep this comparison up until I have a fair sample of trades. I will look for at least 30 trades. This might take six months or more to get a good sample of trades of both methods. I find this comparison trading to be very interesting. It is certainly not boring to me.

And guess what? I actually constantly find improvements in my methods using this technique. I beat my boredom and make more money!

Look, boredom *is* a problem. But it is a problem for only 15 minutes a day or you can even use it as the impetus to make more money like I do!

I think boredom comes partially as a result of discipline. It takes discipline to execute flawlessly. It is boring to be disciplined. I've had students tell me that they wanted to be creative traders. Great! Unfortunately, it is almost impossible to be profitable and creative at the same time.

MAKE SURE TRADING FITS YOUR LIFESTYLE

One of the critical reasons for being a forex trader is the lifestyle that you can lead. All it takes to be a pro forex trader is some capital, an Internet connection, and 15 minutes a day. What you do the rest of the day is up to you.

Trading can be enjoyable. Certainly. And that can be a great reason for you to want to be a trader.

But most people are not interested in trading by itself. They want the results of trading. They want to create a better retirement for themselves. They want to help their parents, friends, and/or their children. They want to pay for their children's education. They want great vacations. They want to travel around the world. They want to do what they want whenever they want!

Stop. Take a few minutes. What lifestyle is your dream? Can you achieve that dream doing what you are doing now? Can you achieve it through forex trading? Few businesses or jobs have the flexibility or ability to create such lifestyle power.

We all have the desire to change our lives. We want to live the life we dream about. We have needs and desires. Forex trading is one of the few ways that you can achieve all this with such little commitment.

I am fortunate enough to live this lifestyle. I wrote this book in the United States, Belize, Singapore, Hong Kong, and Malaysia. I traveled to other countries for pleasure. I traded in all of these countries. I never spent over 15 minutes a day trading forex. That gave me the time to truly live my life. I read a ton of books. I lost 20 pounds recently. I got a great tan. I had a lot of amazing experiences. I saw a lot of unbelievable things. But the key to that lifestyle is that I am a pro forex trader. I can be anywhere and still make money.

You must trade to live, not live to trade. Trading is your tool. Use it.

KEEP YOUR TRADING TO 15 MINUTES A DAY

I recommend trading only 15 minutes a day. This is heretical in the trading community. They usually believe that you should chain yourself to a computer and stare at it all day. Apparently, staring at a screen creates profits. I say it creates a headache.

Sure, day trading can be fun. It can even be profitable. But the big money is made on the big moves. There has never been a day trader who made $100 million. But there are quite a few position traders who have made that much.

I discovered this key to profitable trading through an epiphany I had in the late 1980s. I was trading more than 40 different systems. I was spending all day long feeding my systems. Part of the reasons for using computer-generated systems was to cut down the amount of time trading. Yet here I was spending 12 hours a day making sure that the data were getting entered right, the systems were calculating right, and so on. I realized that I was spending way too much time trading these systems.

I was really getting into the 80/20 Principle, also called the Pareto Principle, at the time. That Principle essentially says that 80 percent of the results of something will come from just 20 percent of the actions. For example, 80 percent of the sales of a company will come from 20 percent of the customers. In this case, 80 percent of the profits were from 20 percent of the systems. Actually, about 90 percent was coming from 10 percent of the systems!

So I cut out 90 percent of my systems and found myself with very little work to do. A little while later, I extended my analysis of my trading and split my trading into two parts: day trading and position trading. Day trading is trading anything under a day and position trading is holding the position over night and usually for a number of days.

What I found shocked me. I found that position trading accounted for over 80 percent of my profits over the year while day trading was less than 20 percent. At the same time, I was spending all day and much of the night day trading, yet it was accounting for only a small percent of my profits!

This analysis forced me to confront the fact that I was really making money on just a few methods that took very little time. I could drop everything and spend just a few minutes a day and yet make almost as much money as I did working all day and most of the night.

Yet something didn't feel right. I was down to trading less than an hour a day, if that. I realized that I felt guilty making so much money but working so little. That damn Puritan work ethic was creeping into my brain! I've worked hard for almost 20 years after this epiphany to overcome this Puritan work ethic feeling but it is still there and I feel a little guilty every time I make money, particularly if it is a lot of money, without doing a lot of work. I know this is irrational, but there you have it.

A few years later, I was speaking to Bruce Babcock about his trading. Bruce was a best-selling futures author, founder of Commodity Traders Consumer Research, and systems designer. In addition, he made a living trading futures, including currency futures. He was one of the smartest traders around. Sadly, he died some time ago.

One of the things that made him so smart was that he spent zero time trading! That's right, zero, nix, nada. What he did was give a copy of his systems to his broker and gave his broker permission to enter the generated signals in the market. Bruce would simply look at his monthly statement to see how he was doing. He never looked at his trading screen. I'm not sure he even had one! My understanding was that he made between 30 percent and 65 percent per year while he was alive "trading" his own account!

Bruce hired a couple of guys to run his business, which left him a lot of time to do only what he really wanted to do, which meant playing golf and tennis every day. He was a pioneer in creating a trading lifestyle. His inspiration helped me to conquer my Puritan work ethic, though not completely.

I did another analysis of my trading and found that my position trading was more profitable when I spend *less* time than if I spent more time. Imagine my shock at this! The difference was not dramatic but it was clear.

I went through another period of soul searching to try to figure out what was going on. I realized that I was creating several problems by spending a lot of time trading.

One problem was that I was overthinking my trades. I was doing the original correct thinking but then I was double guessing myself. I was doing deeper research that was just confusing me. I was looking at everything from every angle. You'd think that would be better but for me it was worse. I have a strong model for analyzing the forex markets. It works. But double guessing myself was creating doubt in my mind without creating any gains in profits or reducing risk. Unfortunately, I was missing a lot of trades and/or getting out too early. I was often suffering from analysis paralysis.

I was raising the trivial to a level of importance. As well as the opposite.

I realized that I was making more money by spending only 15 minutes a day because the time limit forced me to focus only on what was important and kept me from being distracted by sideshows. Limiting the time to only 15 minutes forces me to execute, not think. My focus is to execute flawlessly not to think about what is going on. Execute, don't think! Think some other time. Trading is an act, not a thought. Your thinking should come at another time, without pressure. It should be reflective and focused on making yourself a better trader. But this 15 minutes per day should be completely absorbed with only trading.

Once again, execute, don't think! Heretical, but powerful.

MAKE SURE YOU HAVE ENOUGH CAPITAL

A critical consideration with trading is the amount of capital that you have to trade. What is the right amount to have to trade? The more, the better.

I consider that having $100,000 to start, and using the methods outlined in this book, will ensure that you will be a profitable trader. In fact, you can start with much less.

The real key is to make sure that you have enough capital to have a diversified portfolio yet keep your risk within the limits recommended in this book.

For example, let's assume that you have $5,000 to start trading. Let's say that you are setting your risk limit at 1 percent. That means that you can only risk $50 on a trade. That probably means that you can only trade a micro-account where each pip is worth just 10 cents. A loss of 100 pips is $10, while on a mini-account that would be $100.

The purpose of the micro-account, in this case, is that you can trade just about every signal that comes. You would likely only be able to trade a few trades if you were to be trading a mini-account. Reducing the number of trades will obviously cut the total profits at the end of the year but it also increases risk because your trading profits and losses are focused on fewer trades.

So shift down to a smaller account and give yourself the ability to trade every trade. Over time, you can add money and retain profits and then shift up to a larger account at the appropriate time.

PRIORITY ORDER YOUR METHODS

I like the methods in this order:

1. Channel Breakout
2. Inside Days
3. Trend Analysis
4. Conqueror

5. 20-Day Momentum

6. Reversal Days

I have them in this order to encourage you to implement them in that order. That way, the maximum synergies will emerge. Still, in the final analysis, you should trade those methods that you feel most comfortable with so that you will have the greatest discipline about trading.

FUNDAMENTALS VERSUS TECHNICALS

I never talked about using fundamental analysis to trade the forex market. Frankly, it is too difficult and subtle to teach very well, particularly in a book. In addition, it is not necessary to know the fundamentals to make money. I do teach fundamental analysis to my live students because I can go extensively into the nuances of trading that way.

The good news is that it is not important to know fundamentals to make money trading forex. Fundamentals and technicals can both be profitable or unprofitable. But they have very different attributes.

Fundamentals can be very good at determining the value of a currency pair. Knowing that a pair is worth 1.60 when it is trading 1.40 is very valuable information. Knowing that will cause me to trade that pair only from the long side. Fundamentals can also give us a lot of confidence in our positions because we have a firm understanding of what is going on. In addition, fundamental analysis can enable us to differentiate between different potential trades. "This trade is better than that trade because the fundamentals are more bullish."

But fundamentals have some serious problems. The biggest one is when your analysis is wrong. Then that confidence becomes a deathtrap. That pair is worth 1.60 and the market is 1.40. I should buy. The market moves down to 1.30. I should mortgage my house. The market drifts even lower to 1.20. I should sell my kids. At 1.10, I'm bankrupt. To paraphrase John Maynard Keynes, the market can remain irrational longer than you can remain solvent.

Technicals are also both good and bad. One bad factor is that you can't differentiate between trades. A breakout in two different pairs has to be treated as the same.

The best thing about technical analysis is that it gives you a place to put a stop. And that is very powerful. In fact, that one simple factor is of incredible importance. Let me demonstrate.

I once invented what I called the World's Most Stupid Trading System. It was very simple. I took a period of time of roughly ten years in soybeans.

The rules were that I would buy on the open and place a ten cent trailing stop from the highs. I would buy again on the next day's open if I was stopped out. Simple! Stupid!

As you can imagine, I made money in bull markets because I was only allowed to buy. The market would run for a period of time before I would get stopped out. In bear markets, I lost a lot of money because I was getting stopped out a lot. But the method made money over the whole time frame! The reason was simple. I cut my losses and let my profits run. The simple placement of a stupid arbitrary stop loss was enough to create a profitable system. Another epiphany.

This shows that probably the most significant attribute of technical analysis is the ability to set a reasonable stop loss. In other words, technical analysis allows us to cut our losses and let our profits run.

The ideal trading method would be to combine fundamentals and technicals. Easier said than done.

In the final analysis, if a gun was put to my head, and if I were forced to choose between fundamentals and technicals, I would pick technicals. For the simple reason that it provides clear entry and exit points. This is very important for one's psychology and risk management. As I have mentioned a million times, these are the two most important factors for trading success so the fact that technical analysis supports them better than fundamentals puts me in the technicals camp if I have to choose between the two.

The purpose of all analysis is to put us in tune with the market. We want to understand what the market is telling us and get in sync. That is the only way to make big money.

We cannot and should not fight the market. It is bigger, faster, stronger, and better looking than I am. I will lose all fights. But let me get in tune with the market and I can surf that wave to serious money.

HOW TO PREDICT THE NEWS

I am constantly being asked by my students if they should hold an existing position into a major economic release, such as Non-Farm Payrolls. I always say yes, if there is a clear trend and your trend is in line with the trend. The reason is that it is fairly easy to predict the news! Let me explain.

There is only bullish news in bull markets; only bearish news in bear markets; and a mix in neutral markets! I know, I know, sounds too simple. But take a look at a chart of a major bull market. By definition, most of the news in that period had to be bullish or interpreted by the market as bullish. So you should expect most news to be bullish or at least to be interpreted as bullish.

By holding bullish positions into numbers that should be bullish, you should be gaining incremental profits. Not big money but certainly a greater profit than you would by bailing out of positions before big economic numbers.

The downside is that you will have some bigger swings in the market. In addition, there will be few instances where the news item will create enough volatility that you will be stopped out of your position only to see the market rally after you have been stopped out. Fortunately, this is rare, but it will happen.

In the meantime, you will be gaining a series of small to moderate profits from holding positions into economic news.

The same principle makes it easy to outperform the gurus in predicting the economic numbers. Take the midpoint of predictions and then you should predict something reasonable on the bullish side of predictions. Let's say that the market is predicting a 0.3 percent gain in widget production with 0.2 percent as bullish and 0.4 percent as bearish. It is a bull market in the currency pair you are trading. You should therefore simply make a prediction of, say, 0.1 percent. You will probably be closer to the actual number than the consensus figure of 0.3 percent and therefore make money and be better than economists!

This phenomenon occurs because analysts are always slightly behind reality. They spend their time trying to catch up to what is really going on. Let me prove this.

Let's make just one assumption and that is that analysts and the market have equal ideas of the upcoming number to be released. If the market had perfect prescience then the price of a currency pair would never move because the market would know exactly what is going to happen and would find the correct price for the pair to discount that information. However, note that markets move in waves up and down and sideways. This is the market's attempt to find out the underlying value of the pair.

A trend in a market is caused by the underlying value of a currency pair moving, in this example, higher but the market not seeing the end result. The market therefore churns higher, trying to discount the change in underlying value. It is always behind the value or else there would be a one-time shift to a new higher level.

Therefore, it is easy to predict news items because you are simply capitalizing on the tendency of the analysts to lag the real value of a market. A piece of news comes out, the news is bullish, and the price moves higher.

You will now be able to outperform the gurus who make millions predicting the economic numbers. I suggest that you try this out in the real world and you will see that you will outperform the consensus of predictors. Amazing, but true!

IN CONCLUSION: IS THIS REALLY GUARANTEED TO MAKE MONEY?

Yes.

These are powerful techniques that can create massive profits for you if you follow the rules. I strongly urge you to back-test the ideas in this book to assure yourself that they are profitable. Take a portfolio of the five major pairs and test them over a couple of years. You may not make money in every pair in every year but your total portfolio will make money every year. I am sure of that.

But that is not the critical factor for success. You are.

And, unfortunately, I can't control what you do with the information in this book. I have shown you a lot about psychology and risk management but only you can put them into effect. I stand behind all the ideas in the book but only you can create the massive profits that lay latent within the techniques.

I actually guarantee to my live students that I can make them profitable traders. I will give them back their tuition if they are not profitable over the coming year. I don't teach them much that is different from what is in this book. Guess what? I have yet to refund anyone for failing to make money. This is in spite of the fact that about 90 percent of futures traders lose money.

The advantage I have in live teaching is that I can work closely with my students. I can truly make them something. With you, dear reader, I can only teach you things. You must be the one to put them into action.

I urge you to follow the psychological concepts and risk management rules in this book. They are the hard part. The entry and exit techniques are easy. Putting them into effect is the hard part. You must be consistent and persistent at applying the principles and rules in this book. But you will create significant profits if you do!

You are currently holding a complete package that can seriously enhance your life. Everything in this book has been designed to work with the other parts to present a complete package for making money trading forex. It includes psychology, risk management, and entry and exit rules. Each is important but more important is that you do them all. Leaving out one of these building blocks will cause losses. There is no sense in having great entry and exit rules if you don't use proper risk management and so on.

You now have the opportunity to make massive amounts of money. I look forward to hearing about your success.

Suggested Reading

For any questions, go to www.AskCourtneySmith.com. It's free! I have a few Web sites that contain useful information:

- MaxForexProfits.com: Includes a bonus chapter that will tell you all about the 20-day momentum system developed by Bruce Babcock (maxforexprofits.com/freechapter.html). I've also put a free video on trading channel breakouts there.
- MaxInvestmentProfits.com
- Commodity Trading Consumer Research, located at ctcr.investors.net

I have put together a CD, *The Five Gold Keys of Investment Success*, which contains details about some of the strategies in this book. You may get it for free at http://investmentmentoringinstitute.com/goldkeys/goldkeys.html.

For more information on the psychology of investing, I recommend *Trading in the Zone* (Prentice Hall Press, 2001) by Mark Douglas. It is a *tremendous* book.

For more on designing and testing trading systems, I recommend Bob Pardo's book *The Evaluation and Optimization of Trading Strategies* (John Wiley & Sons, Inc., 2008).

For more information on Tom DeMark, I suggest his first two books, *The New Science of Technical Analysis* (John Wiley & Sons, Inc., 1994) and *New Market Timing Techniques: Innovative Studies in Market Rhythm & Price Exhaustion* (John Wiley & Sons, Inc., 1997).

For more information on Richard Dennis, William Eckardt, and the Turtles, I recommend the book *The Complete Turtle Trader* (HarperBusiness, 2007) by Michael Covel. Michael Covel is also the author of *Trend Following* (FT Press, 2007), which is a more general book on trend following. I recommend it as well.

For more information about Nelson Freeburg and Formula Research, visit www.FormulaResearch.com.

For more information on the Kelly Formula, I highly recommend *Fortune's Formula* (Hill and Wang, 2005). Great information and a great story.

For more information on mentoring to learn how to be a profitable forex trader, please visit www.InvestmentMentoringInstitute.com.

For more information about what I am up to, visit www.CourtneySmith .com.

Acknowledgments

Thanks very much to all the people throughout my life who have helped to get me here.

Thanks to ProRealTime.com for their great charts.

Thanks to George Newhouse for giving me the opportunity to keep on going!

Thanks to Pam for all her support. She knows.

Thanks to the aces at John Wiley & Sons. Pamela van Giessen and Emilie Herman are the best!

Thanks to my parents for all their support throughout the years. You are the greatest!

Thanks to the traders and analysts whose shoulders I stand on in this book. This includes Richard Donchian, Peter Brandt, Magee and Edwards, Colby and Meyers, George Lane, Bob Pardo, Welles Wilder, Bruce Babcock, Larry Williams, and Tom DeMark.

About the Author

C ourtney D. Smith is the chairman of the Investment Mentoring Institute, an organization devoted to building great investors. The Investment Mentoring Institute provides training and mentoring for individual and institutional investors in stocks, futures, and foreign exchange.

He is also president and chief investment officer of Courtney Smith & Co., Inc., which manages money for institutions, family offices, and high-net-worth individuals.

Mr. Smith is the only person in history to manage a highly ranked hedge fund, stock-picking letter, mutual fund, and futures letter.

He was the chief investment officer and chief strategist of Orbitex Management, Inc., during the late 1990s. Orbitex managed mutual funds and portfolios for institutions and individuals.

He was the editor of *Courtney Smith's Wall Street Winners* newsletter. This popular investment advisory newsletter was ranked number one in performance by the Hulbert Digest. Mr. Smith is the owner and editor-in-chief of Commodity Trading Consumer Research (CTCR). CTCR has been providing insight to the futures community since 1983.

Previously, he was president and chief executive officer of Quantum Financial Services, Inc., a futures and stock brokerage firm. Mr. Smith was first vice president and treasurer of the New York branch of Banca della Svizzera Italiana (BSI), a Swiss bank. At BSI, Mr. Smith managed mutual funds and client accounts, and he was responsible for the trading activities of the New York branch as well as trading and marketing fixed income and foreign exchange derivatives for the entire bank. He was also responsible for the funding and balance sheet of the branch.

Mr. Smith was previously group vice president in charge of Financial Derivatives at the French bank Banque Paribas, New York, and was vice president and a director of Research and Commercial Services for PaineWebber, Inc. Mr. Smith managed client accounts prior to joining PaineWebber.

Mr. Smith is the author of five books, including *Profits Through Seasonal Trading* (John Wiley & Sons, 1980), *Commodity Spreads*

(John Wiley & Sons, 1981, and Traders Press, 1989), *How to Make Money in Stock Index Futures* (McGraw-Hill, 1985, paperback edition 1988), *Seasonal Charts for Futures Traders* (John Wiley & Sons, 1987), and *Option Strategies* (John Wiley & Sons, 1987, second edition 1996, third edition 2008). Mr. Smith is also the author of chapters in several books.

Mr. Smith has been a featured speaker at investment conferences throughout North America and Europe. He has appeared on more than one thousand national television shows, such as *Wall Street Journal Report* and *Moneyline,* as well as other shows on CNBC, Fox News, Bloomberg, CNN, and CNNfn.

Index